PATIENTS, PRACTITIONERS, & MEDICAL CARE:

Aspects of Medical Sociology

DAVID ROBINSON
Addiction Research Unit
Institute of Psychiatry
University of London

WILLIAM HEINEMANN MEDICAL BOOKS LTD.

First Published 1973

© David Robinson, 1973

ISBN 0 433 28065 4

Printed and Bound in Great Britain by
Cox & Wyman Ltd.
London, Fakenham and Reading

CONTENTS

Introduction   ix

I. The Sociologist's Viewpoint
Sociology   1
Social action   3
Social relations   4
Social positions and social roles   5
Social groups   11
Sociology and common sense   15
What sociology isn't   16
Summary   17
Suggestions for further reading   18

II. Becoming Ill: a Bio-social Process   19
Sociology and particular illness conditions   20
Differential exposure to illness conditions   27
Health surveys   29
The "clinical iceberg"   33
Differential responses to illness conditions   35
Summary   46
Suggestions for further reading   47

III. The Patient: a Social Position   48
The sick role   52
Exemption from normal social responsibilities   52
The question of responsibility for the illness condition   54
The desire to get well   58
Seeking help   61
Summary   63
Suggestions for further reading   63

IV. Patient and Doctor: a Social Relationship   65
    The patient-doctor relationship   66
    Features of the patient-doctor relationship   69
    Privileged access   73
    The problem of uncertainty   74
    "Non-diseases" and "non-medical problems"   85
    Other experts   80
    Summary   83
    Suggestions for further reading   85

V. Medicine: a particular Profession   87
    Occupations   88
    The prestige of occupations   89
    Professions   92
    Medicine as a particular profession   95
    Autonomy   96
    Recruitment and education   98
    Control   100
    Professionals and para-professionals   103
    Medicine as an institution of social control   106
    Summary   109
    Suggestions for further reading   109

VI. The Hospital: a Complex Organization   111
    Organizations: traditionally defined   111
    Organizations: a more realistic approach   117
    The hospital   119
    The "problem" of communication   125
    Satisfaction with in-hospital information   129
    Questionnaire-based studies   134
    Summary   137
    Suggestions for further reading   138

VII. Sociology and the Provision of Medical Care   139
    The inter-relatedness of medical activities   139
    Referral   142
    Referrals: from medical sources   142

Referrals: from non-medical sources   147
The sociologist in illness situations   152
Unknown observers   153
Known observers   154
Sociology and medicine: a concluding note   159
Suggestions for further reading   160
References   161
Author index   173
Subject index   176

Introduction

"These things one ought to consider most attentively . . . the mode in which the inhabitants live, and what are their pursuits, whether they are fond of drinking and eating to excess, and given to indolence, or are fond of exercise and labour, and are not given to excess in eating and drinking."

Hippocrates, "On Airs, Waters and Places"[1]

The recognition of the close interrelationship between the practice of medicine and the social situation within which that medicine is practised is not new. The Hippocratic corpus points up among other things the importance of considering the social environment as an aetiological factor in disease, and also deals specifically with the doctor-patient relationship as a therapeutic tool. The dazzling scientific advances of the past century may have blinded some to the importance of making an attempt to understand the social concomitants of disease, its presentation, and its management. However, in recent years the insights which were so clearly provided in the classical Greek writings have been re-stressed by both sociologists and the medical profession.

The General Medical Council, in its "Recommendations as to Basic Medical Education"[2] felt that "instruction in the . . . sociological bases of human behaviour . . . should be included". Similarly, the Report of the Royal Commission on Medical Education[3] drew attention to the "steadily increasing realization by doctors of the importance of . . . social factors both in illness itself and in their relationships with their patients". The Royal Commission saw the sociologist being introduced into the medical school as one of a team of representatives from the social and behavioural sciences whose aim should be "to give the student a comprehensive understanding of man in health and sickness and an intimate acquaintance with his physical and social environment". As for the sociologists, the American Sociological Association's section on Medical Sociology was only formed in 1960 yet ten years later had over two thousand members. The equivalent section of the British Sociological Association, formed in 1969, had over 200 members at its 1972 meeting.

The question of what the precise relationship is between medicine and sociology, of what sociologists can actually do in medical schools and what part, if any, they can play in the education of good doctors is frequently asked. It is certainly incumbent upon anyone who inflicts his discipline upon others who have no knowledge of it and whose major interests, by definition, lie elsewhere to make clear what it is that he is trying to do. First of all, is the medical sociologist attempting to turn medical practitioners into "professional sociologists"? Without any hesitation the answer is no. The reason for this is fundamental, and based upon the very nature of the medical enterprise and the essential task of medical education.

The medical student is a potential man of action. That is, he is in the process of becoming a person who will be expected to make decisions, the outcome of which will vitally affect other people. The medical student is not a potential academic. This means that he is not being trained, or encouraged, to specialize in any one discipline. On the contrary he is forced to be exposed to an ever increasing number. Medicine is a synthesis of these many disciplines which leads to the practice of knowledge, skills and attitudes helpful in the care of the sick. George Reader[4] succinctly describes this synthesis when he says:

> There is a certain body of knowledge unique to this activity which might be termed a science of medicine, and which grows by accretion from applications of physical, natural, and social science. Physicians with training in these other disciplines may add to knowledge in the basic science as well as in the applied; by the same token, other scientists may contribute to knowledge in medicine and in their own field as well.

If the sociologist in the medical school is not attempting to produce sociologists what is he trying to do? Very briefly, the sociologist's task is to introduce the notion of man as a social as well as a biological animal, and indicate as clearly and succinctly as possible the relevance and implications of this viewpoint for those whose profession is medicine. That man is a social animal means quite simply that his actions can not be adequately described, much less explained, without understanding and making reference to the social and cultural situation within which he operates. The sociological enterprise is geared to explaining action in particular social situations through gaining an understanding of how the persons involved in that situation see and interpret the world about them. The *medical* sociologist is merely a sociologist whose particular concern is to describe, explain, and indicate implications of, social action in medical and related situations.

Recent changes both in the pattern of disease and in the practice of medicine have rekindled an appreciation of the relevance of the sociological perspective. With the concentration on the germ theory of disease and the spectacular successes of physiological medicine of the "internal environment" there was an understandable tendency to develop medicine as an almost purely biological science. Consequently, medicine's organization and the education of its practitioners reflected this concern. Paradoxically, the very success of this "laboratory tradition" created the need for the approach to be re-thought. The conquest of the major epidemic communicable diseases has radically altered morbidity patterns so that modern medicine is now faced with the less acute but no less demanding problems of chronic and degenerative disorders. This change in the pattern of disease has allowed attention to re-focus on the social concomitants of illness, its presentation, and its management.

Within this broadening perspective it is now possible for the sociologist and the medical practitioner to collaborate in the latter's search for solutions to medical problems. This collaboration is not restricted to such fields as epidemiology, public health and medical administration but is fruitful in all medical specialties where those concerned have an interest in understanding the meaning and implications of any particular illness episode for the symptomatic person, lay and professional others, and the wider society.

Underpinning any particular problem which might exercise the joint attention of sociology and medicine is the mutual realization that the treatment of illness involves more than the application of medical knowledge through formal medical institutions. Those organizations in which the layman receives medical care are closely interrelated with, and supported by, many other bodies and organizations. Local authorities, pharmaceutical companies, various voluntary organizations and the central government all have their part to play in regulating, organizing, and supporting the medical care system. Therefore, the sociologist is concerned, in part, to describe and explain the interrelationships between these medical and non-medical institutions. Similarly, since everyone can be expected to fall ill at some time in their life the sociologist seeks also to explain and illustrate the various lay and professional perspectives through which these illness episodes are viewed. These perspectives will vary according to people's values, beliefs, and experiences of life, and these variations will have implications for the provision and outcome of medical care.

This book seeks to provide a framework within which such concerns can be discussed, and is geared to examining the way in which the sociologist's perspective has implications for and, hopefully, aids the practice of medicine. The value of the collaboration between medicine and sociology for the discipline of sociology is an equally valid concern but will only be touched on in the last chapter.

The application of sociology in medicine is characterized by an orientation to the value of the non-sociologist as well as the sociologist. These values, extrinsic to the discipline of sociology, are regarded by the applied social scientist as legitimate points of orientation for his everyday work. For if the sociologist's insights are to be considered useful by the medical practitioner they must either help to describe more accurately the phases of his dealings with health and illness, or they must increase his ability to predict what he will find as to cause, type of diagnosis, outcome, or success of treatment. In short, they must modify his method of practice in a demonstrably useful way.

One of the difficulties which has confronted the teaching sociologist, his student in the medical school and interested members of the medical professions has been the lack of books written specifically for their situation. Such literature as has been available has tended to be either general medical sociology books giving an outline of the whole field,[5] research monographs by sociologists, on particular aspects of medical care, behaviour, or organization[6] or introductory textbooks on general sociology.[7] However excellent these books may be they were not written for the medical profession. The general medical sociology books and the research monographs demand a prior knowledge of sociology which few medical practitioners or students possess. In addition, they are written primarily to advance sociology as a discipline rather than medicine. The introductory sociology books, on the other hand, while demanding no prior knowledge of the discipline are designed for *potential* sociologists. It has already been pointed out that this is precisely what medical students are not.

This book, therefore, is written primarily for those people who are interested in or concerned with medicine and the provision of medical care. It is hoped, however, that sociologists, medical sociologists, and potential medical sociologists will also find it of interest and use. The aim is to present medically relevant material so that it introduces the distinctive way in which the sociologist sees and interprets the world about him. It is hoped that this way of looking at the world will be seen first, to have relevance for those whose task it is to solve medical problems, and second, to be of interest to all those who seek a better understanding of their position in relation to the medical care system.

The first chapter discusses certain key concepts in order to illustrate "the sociologist's viewpoint", that is, his concern with gaining an interpretive understanding of social action.* The concepts themselves will, by and large, be those used in subsequent discussions of particular topics and problems. Each subsequent chapter will, in fact, concentrate upon one main topic such as the patient, the medical profession, and the hospital. Each of these topics will, as the chapter headings indicate, be used as an example of a particular sociological concern, such as; the patient as a particular social position, medicine as a particular profession, and the hospital as a particular complex organization. After each topic has been introduced the discussion will broaden out to consider the relationship between the particular topic under review and other social phenomena. Material from studies in the field of medical sociology will be introduced, where relevant, to illustrate the particular point being made and also to demonstrate the use and place of certain research methods.

This is an introductory text. It does not attempt to deal with every medical topic which is of interest to the sociologist, or with every topic upon which the medical practitioner might seek to collaborate with the sociologist. However, for those readers whose interest is aroused in either particular topics or the field in general there is a guide to further literature at the end of each chapter.

* Chapter one, outlining the sociologist's viewpoint, need not necessarily be read *before* subsequent chapters. It is intended that each chapter will stand on its own so that readers can either refer to chapter one occasionally for guidance or perhaps when they have completed the other chapters.

CHAPTER I

The Sociologist's View-point

*"Medicine is a social science in
its very bone and marrow."*

Rudolph Virchow, 1849[1]

Sociology is the study of man in society, but there is nothing
very novel in that. Men have always analysed and attempted
to understand various aspects of the societies and groups in
which they lived.

Similarly, to say that sociology is concerned with man in
society in no way helps us to understand what sociology is, or
what sociologists do. It is rather like saying that medicine is
concerned with health and illness. This is true but does not tell
us anything about what medical science is or what medical
practitioners do. A further problem with saying that sociology
is concerned with man in society is that there are other
disciplines such as economics, politics and law, to which the
phrase applies equally well. Given all this it would be very
reasonable to demand at the outset a definition of sociology
which would set out clearly and simply its essential and distinguishing features. This, however, immediately raises the
unavoidable problem of specialist language. How useful would
it be to say to someone who is just beginning to seek an acquaintance with the discipline that sociology "attempts to develop
an analytic theory of social action systems in so far as these
systems can be understood in terms of common value integration"?[2] Clearly, this definition only has meaning to someone
who already has an adequate grasp of the terms "social
action", "system" and "common value integration". Whether
we would want to accept such a definition, even if we did have
a grasp of the terms, is a further but separate question. But to
understand what it is that a person is doing when he is "being

a sociologist" it is necessary to build up a working knowledge of the basic concepts with which he operates. This is not, of course, a difficulty peculiar to sociology but is a fundamental feature of any discipline. The introduction referred to sociologists "making sense of the world about them". The concepts of a discipline are the tools with which any scientist, whether he is a sociologist, a biochemist or an anatomist, organizes and interprets those things in the world about him which are his discipline's particular concern.

Although all disciplines have their special language and concepts with which they focus attention upon selected aspects of the world there is a tendency, particularly in the social sciences, for this specialist language to proliferate unnecessarily. When this happens the special language is termed jargon, which is merely the pejorative term for someone else's special language! However, this book will keep the use of specialist terms and concepts as controlled as is consistent with being able to introduce and demonstrate the sociologist's viewpoint.

Although sociology is concerned with men in society it is evident that all we see about us are individuals, some of whom are known to us personally, some known by sight or reputation, and some not known at all. How, then, does the sociologist transform a consideration of the individuals who happen to inhabit the world about him at any particular time into a coherent understanding of groups of men, institutions or societies? The remainder of this chapter sets out what it is about men in society which is of peculiar interest to the sociologist.

Sociology

Sociology is one of the social sciences and an understanding of this adjective "social" is crucial to an appreciation of what sociology is. Unfortunately, the use of the word is as loose as it is widespread. At the end of the last century the French sociologist Emile Durkheim wrote that the use of the word "social" to apply to "practically all phenomena generally diffused within a society however small their social interest" meant that "there are, as it were, no human events that may not be called social".[3]

It would be possible to spend the whole of this book setting out an account of the intricacies and minor sophistications of sociologists' arguments and discussions with each other about the precise shades of meaning attached to various key concepts. But that is not our present purpose. Rather our interest is with those major features of the discipline which offer a distinctive approach to the study of medical problems. A fruitful way of beginning to outline this approach is to turn to Max Weber's discussion of social action and social relations. This will reveal the crucial notion of "the social" and also provide a firm foundation upon which the remaining discussion can be built.

Social action

Weber's outline of the distinctive difference between social and non-social action lies, disguised to a greater or lesser extent, at the heart of all subsequent sociological theories. Writing at the turn of the century,[4] he defined social action as action "oriented towards the past, present or expected future behaviour of others". The "others" to whom we are oriented may be known or unknown or may constitute an "indefinite plurality". As an example of this latter possibility, "an indefinite plurality", Weber cites the exchange of money. In this activity an individual's behaviour is guided by the expectation that an indefinite and unspecific number of others will accept money as a means of exchange. The money-user does not know all the other people but his action is informed by an expectation of the way in which they will behave.

The notion of *expectations about others' actions* and the way in which these expectations inform an individual's actions is the very core of the sociologist's concern. His business is to offer explanations of social actions in specific social situations, and he can only do this by first of all gaining a clear understanding of the values, beliefs and expectations which inform and guide these actions. The way in which the sociologist actually goes about investigating and trying to delineate people's values, beliefs and expectations is an allied and equally fundamental question. However, the use of particular methods and techniques will not be dealt with in this chapter but introduced later when their relevance for providing data about particular medical situations and concerns can be demonstrated.

Upon the basic notion of social action are built all the other concepts which we shall discuss. Since social action is action oriented towards the conduct of others it is essential to construct a framework within which to analyse relationships between people. Social relations are the smallest unit with which the sociologist is concerned when he begins to construct his concept of society. In fact, whenever sociologists attempt to offer a definition of the term society they usually introduce some phrase like "networks of social relations".

Social relations

To return to Weber, he sees the term social relations referring to the situation where two or more persons are engaged in conduct wherein "in its meaningful content, the action of each takes account of that of the other and is oriented in these terms". The social relation thus consists of the probability that individuals will behave in some meaningfully determined way. The word "meaningfully" here signifies that there is some subjective understanding on the part of the participant actors of each other's behaviour. We thus come back again to the notion of "expectations" which is, as Rex says, "the key category in the definition of social relations".[5] Rex goes on to say that "if we can show that any individual will act in a certain way", then "we are usually justified in speaking of the existence of social relation".

This definition of a social relation merely outlines its general characteristic. Its content, as Weber states, may be "most varied: conflict, hostility, sexual attraction, friendship, loyalty or market exchange; it may involve the fulfilment or evasion or severance of an agreement; economic, erotic or any other form of competition; a sharing of occupations or membership in the same class or nation". Given all this it is legitimate to demand that the discussion be made more specific. Who are "the individuals" and who are "the others" of whom the individuals have expectations which orient their actions? The first thing to say in answer to this question is that the sociologist is concerned with people but not specific people. That is, he is not primarily interested in Mrs Jones *as* Mrs Jones, but rather Mrs Jones in so far as she is seen, and sees herself, to occupy certain social positions.

Social positions and social roles

Every person, however unique we may feel them to be when we live with them, treat them, consult them, work with them, or in some way know them intimately, shares certain characteristics with other people. We can, thus, catagorize people according to whether or not they share any *particular* characteristic. For instance, we may categorize people according to some shared biological characteristic such as "having red hair", or some shared physiological characteristic such as "being over six feet tall", or some shared clinical characteristic such as "having breast cancer".

Shared characteristics may also be social, and these are the ones which most concern the sociologist. Individuals share certain social characteristics in that they are seen to occupy the same social position *vis-à-vis* certain other people. For example, from the wider biological category of "female" we can extract a narrower social category whose shared characteristic is that they occupy the social position of "mother". This characteristic is considered social, rather than merely biological, in so far as it refers to the fact that people have expectations about the way mothers should behave. Just as non-mothers have ideas about the way mothers should behave so mothers themselves have ideas about the way they ought to behave *as mothers*. In any particular situation the way in which a specific mother's behaviour is evaluated will depend upon how much coincidence there is between her idea of the way she should behave as a mother and the expectations of the "others" in the situation.

It is customary in the literature of sociology to speak of these bundles of expectations as a social role. This is a very commonly used notion and will be referred to again in subsequent chapters. The relationship between social position and social role is intimate. A person occupies a social position in relation to other people in a related set of positions. In the family the position of mother is clearly related to other positions such as father, daughter, and son. These clusters of related positions constitute social groups, which will be defined and discussed later in the chapter. If social position is thought of as a place occupied by people *vis-à-vis* other people in related positions, then social role represents the dynamic aspect of behaviour associated with a social position. Mother is a social position. The mother's role is the way in which a person occupying the social position of mother expects and is expected to behave. But the drama analogy must not be taken too far. There is no authorized script for social life.

Not everyone agrees, of course, about what is the appropriate behaviour for someone who occupies any particular social position. Delineating and offering explanations for disagreement or conflict over social expectations is one of the sociologist's primary tasks. His concern is also to outline the implications of these disagreements and conflicts for those whose concern is to understand and to solve certain practical problems. Conflicts about appropriate behaviour are of two main types. First there are those conflicts which arise when two or more people disagree about what is the proper way for someone occupying a certain social position to behave. Such disagreements can have many causes. People's ideas may change over time, while people's different social or cultural backgrounds, or different experiences may cause them to disagree. To return to the family example, it would be unlikely that many mothers from the eighteenth century would agree with many mothers today about the way mothers ought to bring up their teenage daughters. Similarly, the mothers of Surbiton would probably disagree with the mothers of Tibet over their rights and duties as mothers. These are clear and obvious instances of likely disagreements over appropriate behaviour, but it is certainly not necessary to draw upon such extreme examples. Within every family at certain times there are conflicts, of varying degrees of intensity, about what is the "proper" way to behave. When children grow up and are exposed to an ever-widening variety of experiences and situations they may modify their ideas about what, for example, a mother can be expected to do or not do. A daughter's plea that "everybody else's mother allows them to stay out until midnight" can be thought of on the one hand as merely a bit of special pleading on the daughter's part to get her own way. In addition, however, it can be seen as an example of the universal tendency to categorize people according to their social positions. Behind the daughter's plea, there is the assumption that if someone else's mother does something then it is legitimate to claim that one's own mother, because she shares that social characteristic, should do the same.

The use of social categories is one of the ways in which we make the leap from considering known unique individuals in particular to dealing with societies or the human race in general. It must be stressed again, though, that this process of categorization and classification is not a peculiar trait of the sociologist but is something which we all do all the time. We are always classifying people according to the social positions which they occupy and then making judgments about their actions in the light of the expectations *we* have about the way people occupying those positions ought to behave.

The second type of conflict over appropriate behaviour stems from the fact that everyone possesses many social characteristics and can therefore occupy many social positions. A person occupying the social position of mother in our continuing example may also occupy the positions of wife, daughter, and sister. Rights and duties will be perceived to be associated with occupying each of these other positions. For the most part the various roles which the person plays may be quite compatible with each other, but this is by no means certain or guaranteed.

Let us take the case of a person who is a mother of young children and who is also employed. She occupies the social positions of both mother and employee, and the duties which she and or others see to be associated with these two roles might well conflict. If her young child falls ill, for example, and has to be admitted to hospital there may be a conflict between, on the one hand, fulfilling what she sees to be her role as a mother, by making every effort to be at the hospital during visiting times, and, on the other hand, of fulfilling her role as an employee, by making every effort to be regularly at work during those hours when she is expected and paid to be there. The conflict is not over differing ideas about the way a person occupying a particular social position ought to behave but rather over the incompatible demands of adequately performing the roles associated with occupying two different social positions.

Both types of conflict are, of course, very common. The sociologist's concern is in part to indicate and suggest the implications of such conflicts for those who must solve particular problems in specific social situations. The sociologist with a particular interest in medicine might very well be concerned with the implications of the conflict inherent in the working mother's situation. His work might then be of use to those who have to plan for, administer, or work in hospitals in which there are sick children.

Recent studies of mothers' attitudes and behaviour in relation to the hospitalization of their young children[6] were designed to throw light on just this particular problem. The impetus for these studies came from the realization that the recommendations of the Platt Committee[7] concerning "The Welfare of Children in Hospital" were not easily being implemented. The Platt recommendations which attracted most attention were those concerned with unrestricted visiting and mothers-in units. There was a widespread belief, before the studies were carried out, that mothers' home commitments were not really an inhibitor to taking advantage of the proposed unrestricted-visiting and living-in facilities. MacCarthy,[8] for example, in reply to Meadow's[9] suggestion that mothers would be less likely to live in if they had other children at home, asserted that when the hypothetical situation of having a child hospitalized becomes a reality "it is likely that in the face of a genuine offer" mothers will "master their anxieties and make less of their home difficulties". Another paediatrician, Riley,[10] made a similar point, in a discussion of the use of his mother-in unit at Stobhill General Hospital, Glasgow, when he said that "a large family need be no barrier".

However, if a mother is to take advantage of unrestricted visiting and living-in facilities, she must feel that doing so is of sufficient importance to let it take priority over other home commitments. From the study material there was evidence that few mothers felt that being with a young hospitalized child was of prime importance. When asked about priorities, mothers were quite definite about the greater importance of work and education commitments, and could not visualize calling upon anyone other than their mothers and mothers-in-law to help out if, in response to a hypothetical question, they were to imagine themselves "going to live in hospital with a sick child tomorrow". Neighbours and friends were rarely mentioned as potential sources of help. Several mothers said that they would not like to ask neighbours and friends "for this kind of thing". Even among a sample of mothers who had, in fact, lived in, two-thirds gave as their main reason for doing so the fact that they were asked to go in by the hospital.

Quite apart from mothers, in general, feeling that living-in or visiting for long periods was not important enough to make the necessary arrangements for the adequate maintenance of the normal running of the family, some mothers held ideas about child rearing quite inconsistent with those notions of child mental health which underpinned the Platt report. Several felt that a period of separation may be a good opportunity for a young child to learn to stand on its own feet.

As the mother of one two-year-old boy put it, "there's no point, (in living-in), it wouldn't make him any better. Anyway, they've got to stand on their own feet, it's never too young to start training them."

Home commitments clearly influence the readiness with which a mother will visit or live in with her young child in hospital. But it is the mother's notions of appropriate behaviour which make her put other family commitments before being with a sick child; notions of the appropriate amount of independence in young children, and notions of who it is appropriate to call to help in crisis situations. Mothers will need to have the value and importance of being with their child in hospital pointed out to them if they are to take advantage of facilities which at present seem to most of them merely a cause of a certain amount of personal inconvenience. When children are ill, mothers perform the role of nurse in the home. If the illness warrants it, then the child goes to hospital where it is looked after by professional nurses. Although it is accepted that, on occasions, the professionals come into the home to guide the mother in her nursing duties (i.e. G.P.s and the few Home Care Units), there is certainly no tradition of "home" and "professional" nurses joining forces in the hospital situation as the Platt report hoped they would.

As a result of this kind of evidence it became clear that if the Platt recommendations were to be effectively implemented then either parents would have to be persuaded to take advantage of the facilities which have been increasingly provided in recent years or other people, such as, for example, play leaders, would have to be introduced into the ward in an attempt to provide substitutes for maternal support when the young child is hospitalized.

This digression has attempted to show how the approach of the sociologist, whose concern is with delineating and understanding the meaning and significance of particular social situations for the various people involved, might aid those whose task is to solve problems in the field of medicine and medical administration. The digression arose out of a discussion of the fact that any one person occupies many social positions in relation to each of which he and others have ideas, though not necessarily the *same* ideas, about what counts as appropriate behaviour.

Social groups

In everyday conversation the term *group* is used to apply to many different collectivities of people. Medical students are likely to be spoken of as a group, so are grave diggers, the members of a family, the Cabinet, people earning over £5,000 a year, bus drivers, readers of *The Times*, women, people with broken legs, members of a working men's club, admirers of Jane Fonda, patients, and so on. Obviously it would be difficult to characterize all these various entities in a general way. The sociologist, thus, tends to define a social group rather more precisely in order to distinguish it from other forms of collectivity.

Given that the sociologist is concerned with a study of social action and social relations, a social group is commonly defined along the following lines as: "a number of people whose relationships are based upon a set of inter-related roles and social positions, who share certain beliefs and values, and who are sufficiently aware of their shared or similar values to be able to differentiate themselves from other people". According to this definition we would class the members of a family, the Cabinet, and the members of a working men's club as "social groups". On the other hand, women, bus drivers, grave diggers, and patients would be "social categories" made up of persons occupying similar social positions, while people earning over £5,000 a year, readers of *The Times*, and admirers of Jane Fonda would be merely "statistical aggregates". That is, they merely possess some social attribute by virtue of which they can be logically classed together.

Although social categories and statistical aggregates have been distinguished from social groups it is quite possible for them to emerge *as* social groups. The mechanisms and implications of such an emergence is something which the

sociologist would want to study. For example, one of Jane
Fonda's admirers in Bradford might put a notice in the
Telegraph and Argus calling for all like-minded people to contact
him with a view to forming a local Jane Fonda fan club to act
as a forum for discussing the relative merits of that lady as
opposed to Brigitte Bardot. The resultant Jane Fonda Appreciation Society (Bradford branch) would be a social group.
The people involved would occupy related positions in the
organization such as chairman, secretary, treasurer, projec-
tionist, committee member, club member and so on, they
would share certain beliefs and values concerning, for example,
aesthetics and film making, and they would be aware of their
common bond with each other and appreciate that this
differentiated them from other people.

This rather frivolous example merely indicates the distinction between a statistical aggregate and a social group and how
the former may become the latter. In the field of medicine the
emergence of various patients' associations exemplifies similar
processes. Patients, from being merely a social category of
people who occupied a similar position *vis-à-vis* other positions
in the medical system, have recently become organized to a
certain extent. Similarly, the various associations concerned
with the welfare of children in hospital are social groups which
developed out of the belief that people who occupied a similar
social position, that of parent of a young hospitalized child,
had interests in common and needed some kind of formal
machinery to make these interests known. It would now be
impossible to understand the workings of the modern hospital
system in Britain without paying attention to the relationships
between the various professional and lay groups, such as those
just mentioned, which go to make up that system.

Certainly some social groups are more important than others.
The Bradford branch of the Jane Fonda Appreciation Society
may be of vital importance to its members but it is likely to
have little importance for anyone outside Bradford, even Jane
Fonda. The Cabinet, on the other hand, is a social group of the
greatest importance irrespective of the particular people who

compose it at any one time. Its importance derives from the fact that it occupies a strategic position in that related set of groups and activities which go to make up the political system. The political system is, of course, one of the more enduring elements of social activity and such elements command special attention.

We all occupy positions in many social groups, some of which overlap. A person who is a father in one social group may be a general practitioner in another, a golf club member in a third, a freemason in a fourth, and so on. His activities in each social group will be informed by the expectations and values of that group. This question of group values is crucial, therefore, to any understanding of social action in any particular situation since men's beliefs and values are their way of making sense of these situations.

If the sociologist wants to offer an explanation for why a given group acts in a particular way at a particular time he must refer to those ideas which are available to the group at that time. These ideas will in part determine what the group will *choose* to do. Similarly, the sociologist must refer to and take account of the conditions actually prevailing at the time in question since they, of course, determine what it is *possible* to do. As a separate question he might want to offer some historical explanation for why those particular ideas and conditions are as they are.

In addition to his concern with relations within social groups the sociologist is interested in the relations of one group with another. Such an investigation is an essential prerequisite, in fact, to his offering an explanation of social action within any specific social situation. The position of a group within a complex of groups may be said to determine the social conditions of action of the group concerned. This relates to the earlier point, which stressed that if we want to offer an explanation for the way a group behaves at a particular time we shall have to refer to the ideas which happen to be available at that time. We all occupy many positions, but when we occupy a position in one particular setting we do not ignore those beliefs and values which inform our activities in other settings. People, thus, bring to their activities in any specific situation the beliefs and values which inform their activities in those other situations in which they participate.

Therefore, whether we are sociologists or members of the medical profession, it is an essential prerequisite to an understanding of social action in medical settings to know to which other groups the people we are concerned with belong, what values and beliefs inform their behaviour in those groups, what demands are made upon them, how compatible are their goals in those other groups with their goals in the groups to which they belong in the medical system, and so on.

Before ending this discussion on the concepts of social position, social role and social group, it is essential to get one thing absolutely clear. It is not being maintained or even suggested that society is made up of a structure of groups of related positions, which we all agree upon, associated with each of which are sets of social roles, which again we all agree upon. Nothing could be further from the truth as is clear from giving a moment's thought to the many disagreements which we all have about "the appropriate person" to do something or "the appropriate way" of doing it. The notions social group, social position and social role are useful in that they correspond with the way in which many people tend to conceptualize the society in which they live. But it can *not* be over-emphasized that while you or I may construct all kinds of structures of related groups of positions and associated roles in order to make sense of the world about us there is no *one* structure or *one* set of positions which will encompass and accommodate all our particular constructions. The sociologist's task, as has been pointed out before, is to tease out, to describe, to explain, and to indicate the implications of the fact that we all *differ*, to a greater or lesser extent, in the way in which we each of us categorize, structure, and, thus, make sense of the social world about us. This leads us straight to another question which it is essential to be clear about as soon as possible; the relationship between sociology and common sense.

Sociology and common sense

One of the most common attacks upon sociology is that it deals with the obvious and the common-sensical. If the sociologist writes or says something with which the layman agrees it is likely to be dismissed as being "obvious". On the other hand if the sociologist writes or says something with which the layman disagrees, or describes something which does not accord with the layman's experience, it is likely to be dismissed as "a generalization which does not square with reality" at best, or at worst just plain "wrong". Some sociologists get depressed by this double-bind situation. Their despair, however, stems from their rather unhelpful positivistic stance in relation to the common-sense interpretations of social life. They have forgotten that no sociologist worth his salt could possibly imagine for a moment that his discipline, as a *social* science, could be anything if not grounded in the various common-sense worlds of everyday understanding.

Because we are all social and thinking animals we are all committed to understanding our everyday social lives. We all have ideas and theories about the way in which our lives work and are ordered, about what matters to people and what makes them do what they do, about what implications the actions of certain people have for them, for us, and for the wider society. Social life is in essence this understanding, interpreting, attempting to control, bargaining over, theorizing about, anticipating, learning from, and being mistaken over the causes and consequences of our own actions and the actions of others. Each person is, thus, his own sociologist acting in any situation in response to the facts as he sees them and in terms of the ideas, beliefs and theories which order for him those common-sense facts of his everyday life.

It is clear then that the sociologist can never make any claims to describe social action, much less to explain or set out the implications of it in relation to any particular situation, unless he is aware of and intimately understands the *"everyday sociologies"* in terms of which action in that situation is ordered. Any "professional" sociology which is not grounded in a systematic study of the common-sense meanings and actions of everyday life will, quite simply, bear no meaningful relationship to the social world.

The key difference between the "professional" and the "everyday" sociologist is that the former attempts to build upon common-sense interpretations in order to obtain a more general trans-situational understanding of social life. His task is to abstract common themes, to hypothesize from a knowledge of action in one situation about what he will find in another apparently similar situation, and to theorize about what he finds where he finds it.

The sociologist's theories of social action may be very grand, complex and high-powered. But however grand they are, the basic subject matter upon which he builds and to which he returns to substantiate his theories are those common-sense understandings of everyday life in terms of which we all, as *social* beings, operate.

What sociology isn't

The sociologist is a student of man in society. But, however much his work may be used and of use to other people, his specialized knowledge and approach does not qualify him to be society's doctor, or priest or planner. Neither the sociologist nor the non-sociologist should inflate the discipline's sphere of competence. Durkheim sought to make the distinction between sociology and social doctrine as explicit as possible when he said, in The Rules of Sociological Method, that "sociology . . . will be neither individualistic, communistic, nor socialistic. . . . On principle it will ignore those theories, in which it could not recognize any scientific value, since they tend not to describe or interpret but to reform social organization."[11] Other sociologists have spent a great deal of time warning their colleagues about the danger of personal sentiments leading them to report not "what is" but "what ought to be".

Clearly as a member of the human race the sociologist will have his own ideas, values, biases and viewpoints relating to the things going on around him. But when he is occupying the social position of sociologist Weber, for example, urges that his work should be "value free". As a citizen his interests and values might draw him to certain areas and cause him to be curious about particular issues, but the conduct and presentation of his work as a sociologist must follow the broad rules and conventions of scientific procedure. However, there are those who would claim that the sociologist's task is to be critical of the *status quo*. Robert Lynd in a stimulating essay "Knowledge for What?"[12] urges the social sciences "to be troublesome, to disconcert the habitual arrangements by which we manage to live along, and to demonstrate the possibility of change in more adequate directions". Certainly, any piece of social investigation by revealing certain facts of social existence may undermine cherished beliefs or question long established truths. However, it is not the sociologist's aim *as a sociologist* to achieve this, any more than it is his aim to comfort, or approve, or acclaim.

This chapter has attempted to show what it is about man in society that the sociologist is particularly concerned with. Subsequent chapters will discuss specifically medical topics in order to demonstrate the way in which the sociologist approaches this particular aspect of social life.

Summary

The aim of this chapter has been to introduce some aspects of the sociologist's perspective when he attempts to make sense of the world about him. At the core of all sociological theories is the notion of *social action* which Weber defined as action "oriented towards the past, present or expected future behaviour of others".[13] This notion of *expectations about others' actions*, and the way in which such expectations inform the action of particular categories of people in particular situations lies at the heart of the sociologist's concern.

The danger of overstating the drama analogy was indicated. For while the idea of social role is useful it should *not* be taken to imply that individuals are, or should be, performing scripted roles in accordance with some grand societal screenplay. There is no director of society ensuring uniformity and social inter-relatedness. We are all directors. That is, we all have expectations about the way in which we and others can, and should, and possibly will, behave who occupy certain social positions such as patient, doctor, prostitute or prime minister. It follows from this that it is unhelpful to seek for *the* correct script for someone who occupies a particular social position, or to expect there to be universal or even widespread agreement about the way the role should be played.

It is precisely because this is so that there is such a thing as sociology at all. For sociology, whether "professional" or "lay", is our way of making sense of the social world about us. It attempts to describe, offer explanations, and indicate the implications of, people's differing ideas about appropriate behaviour in the light of people's membership of social groups and the ways in which those groups are organized and related to each other. The difference between the "professional" and the "lay" sociologist is that the former tries to build upon everyday sociologies in order to make testable trans-situational generalizations.

Suggestions for further reading:

Berger, P. *Invitation to Sociology*. Penguin Books, Harmonds-worth, 1963.

Coulson, M.A. and Riddell, D.S. *Approaching Sociology: a critical introduction*. Routledge and Kegan Paul, London, 1970.

Worsley, P. *et al. Introducing Sociology*. Penguin Books, Har-mondsworth, 1971.

Worsley, P. *et al.* (eds). *Modern Sociology: introductory readings*. Penguin Books, Harmondsworth, 1971.

Worsley, P. *et al.* (eds). *Problems of Modern Society: a sociological perspective*. Penguin Books, Harmondsworth, 1972.

CHAPTER II

Becoming Ill: a Bio-social Process

"The morbid episodes of life – symptoms, illnesses, disabilities as well as their attempted cures – cannot be regarded as purely physiological processes. Their full understanding requires a systematic consideration of the social and psychological context in which the episodes occur."
John Kosa, 1966[1]

Everybody can expect to fall ill at some time in their lives since no-one is immune from all diseases, disabilities and disorders. In fact illness conditions are everyday facts of life which we all live with, or consult about, or treat, or see in other people, or pass judgment on, or fear, or ignore, or take precautions against.

The sociologist's concern with illness, however, is not merely a concern with illness conditions. The distinction must be stressed at the outset between the possession of some symptom or illness condition and concomitant behaviour. The distinction is between disease, illness condition, disability, symptoms, disorder on the one hand, and "being ill" on the other. Mechanic[2] labelled the concern with the behavioural concomitants of illness conditions the study of "illness behaviour". This he defined as "the way in which given symptoms may be differentially perceived, evaluated, and acted (or not acted) upon by different kinds of persons".

The attempt to understand illness behaviour is not a purely academic pursuit. In addition it has relevance for those whose task is to treat illness conditions or to provide and administer medical services. As Mechanic points out:

> whether we are concerned ourselves with the necessary conditions for building etiological theories or those for bringing

treatment to those most in need of such help, it is necessary that we understand the influence of a variety of norms, values, fears, and expected rewards and punishments on how a symptomatic person behaves.

In short:

the realm of illness behaviour falls logically and chronologically between two major concerns of medical science: etiology and therapy. Variables affecting illness behaviour come into play prior to medical scrutiny and treatment, but after etiological processes have been initiated. In this sense illness behaviour even determines whether diagnosis and treatment will begin at all.

This extended quotation raises two major questions. First, why does one person rather than another contract illness condition X? Second, why does one person rather than another consult a doctor about illness condition X? The first question has traditionally exercised these working in the fields of epidemiology, public health, and social, preventive and occupational medicine. Their task has been to plot the distribution of diseases, and to pinpoint those people most "at risk" to particular diseases or illness conditions because of the way they live or the work which they do. The medical sociologist, on the other hand, tends to be more oriented towards the second question. He wants to offer explanations for why people behave in the way they do irrespective of the particular illness condition which they possess, or to which they are exposed.

Sociology and particular illness conditions

Although the sociologist is concerned to explain the way people behave irrespective of the particular illness conditions which they consider themselves or are considered by others to possess he does, in addition, have things to say about particular diseases. However, in order to ensure that we do not entertain unrealistic expectations about the role of the sociologist it is essential to be quite clear from the outset about which questions in relation to particular illnesses he can be expected to address himself to, and which he can not. A brief digression may help to identify the distinction.

Let us assume that we want, as members of the medical profession, as governments, or as human beings, to tackle "the problem of obesity". In order to do so we would want to have answers to such straightforward questions as "what makes people fat" or "why is X fatter than Y?" For, if we can satisfactorily answer these questions we might then be in a position to realistically legislate, advise, treat or whatever, in order to prevent or cure obesity and its related problems. Clearly many disciplines and sciences might tackle the problem and come up with answers to the straightforward questions which we have posed.

For example, it might be thought that the reason why some people are fat while others are thin is intimately associated with cellular glucose uptake. If this is the case then the sociologist has nothing to contribute to this area of study. He has no theory of cellular glucose uptake, nor can he construct one from the social phenomena which are his basic subject matter. It is within the brief of other disciplines to offer explanations for why some people have a greater muscle glucose uptake than other people thus enabling them to divert ingested carbohydrate away from adipose tissue. In other words it is not the sociologist's task to account for the metabolic patterns which appear to distinguish the lean person from the fat person. This is not to say, however, that there are not other intimately related questions, of their nature sociological, which it might be essential to consider if we are concerned to understand and explain why some people are obese while others are not, or why some people eat more carbohydrates than others.

For example, given two sets of people of similar metabolism we might want to offer explanations for why one set eats more and is fatter than the other. Explanations of such differences might be offered in terms of divergent conceptions of what the two sets consider is, for them, appropriate behaviour in relation to food, or different ideas about what constitutes a "good" or "desirable" figure, or in response to the requirements of differing life styles, or in terms of food rituals, or religious observances, or level of physical activity demanded by the occupany of differing familial or occupational positions, and so on. These are all questions about social actions, relations and beliefs which might attract the attention of the sociologist and which, as a result, may enable him to make statements of more or less generality about why particular people in particular situations are considered or consider themselves fat, and about the social implications of their "fatness". Thus, a theory of cellular glucose uptake and a theory of food rituals will both produce legitimate but *different* answers to the common-sense question of why some people are fatter than others. It is then up to the medical profession, the legislator or the administrator to act in the light of these different but legitimate theories of "fatness" in order that obesity and related medical problems may be prevented, cured, or made more unlikely, reduced or alleviated.

It has been seen that the sociologist may offer a strand in an overall explanation of why a particular condition, such as obesity, develops. However, the sociologist does not, any more than the medical professional, take for granted what is to count as "obesity". For any analysis of being a patient is intimately related to an analysis of what will count as "having" a particular illness condition.

Let us assume that we wanted to say something about the process of becoming an alcoholic. In relation to any particular professional or lay person or persons in any particular medical or non-medical situation it would be necessary to have some understanding of what counts for those people as "being an alcoholic" or "having alcoholism". Any explanation or description of particular people in particular situations which did not attempt to tease out these taken-for-granted assumptions would be unsatisfactory as sociology and unhelpful or misleading for the medical professional since it would, clearly, not bear any meaningful relation to the particular social action under discussion.

It is, of course, not necessary to "do some formal sociology" in order to make sense of every particular action in any situation. Our own common-sense assumptions whether we are sociologists or medical professionals will carry us through. We assess particular signs, we have an immense amount of information and everyday theory about the human actors we meet in normal life. We have theories of motives which enable us to explain to ourselves the motives of others in order to better anticipate or control what they will do and in order to respond sensibly to them. As Douglas[3] puts it:

> In this sense, each man is necessarily his own sociologist; and *everyday sociology* is an extremely complex set of facts, ideas, theories, ideologies, and philosophies demanding expert knowledge of those who would practice it well.

The relationship between such complex common-sense sociologies, in terms of which we each of us order and make sense of the world about us, and the discipline of sociology was discussed in the previous chapter. The academic as opposed to everyday sociology is concerned to gain an understanding of members' "everyday sociologies of their situations" and then to create trans-situational knowledge.

It is clear from this that while certain aspects of medical knowledge may be shared across situations by members of the medical profession, by virtue of a shared training or experience, other aspects of the professional's ideas about medicine will not be shared by all professionals. If this is the case among professionals how much more likely it is to be the case that there will be discrepancies between the professional's and the layman's notions of what sign counts as a symptom of a particular disease, or what is the appropriate response to it.

To illustrate some of these points let us continue our consideration of "what is alcoholism?" Where alcohol is known rules for its use and for abstention are prescribed, usually in fine detail. There appear to have been very few, if any, societies whose people knew the use of alcohol and yet paid little attention to it.[4] Alcohol may be tabooed, it is not ignored. But while alcohol and rules for its use may be almost universal facts of social life, those at all familiar with the academic or professional literature concerned with alcohol-related problems will readily agree with Mulford that:

> Researchers and clinicians alike have difficulty identifying alcoholics and diagnosing alcoholism. Specific criteria for sorting 'real alcoholics' from non-alcoholics are not merely indefinite: they are virtually non-existent.[5]

The problen of agreeing precise definitions and diagnostic criteria is not, of course, specific to notions related to alcohol. As Wing says of the functional psychoses:

> Insufficient is known about the concomitant physiological dysfunctions to allow an objective classification to be made, and diagnosis rests solely upon the skill of the clinician in eliciting present and past symptomatology, interpreting any clues as to causation, and applying the rules of classification he had been taught in the school of psychiatry to which he belongs.[6]

What to include in any scheme of medical classification is a difficult problem, However, it is essential to be clear not only about the logical justification for subsuming some sign, disorder, disturbance or action, under some categorical heading but also about what implications such subsumption has, both for the professional and for the laymen.[7]

In respect of alcoholism there has been a discernible and well-documented[8] shift over the past century from considering it as primarily a legal or moral problem;

> . . . a sin, heinous and soul-wrecking, whose victims shall not possess the Kingdom of Heaven.[9]

to considering it primarily as one of medicine or public health:

> . . . a psychogenic dependence on, or a physiological addiction to, ethanol manifested by the inability . . . consistently to control either the start of drinking or its termination once started. . . .[10]

But, as Edwards points out:

> . . . much of the necessary evidence on which to make a decision as to whether alcoholism is a disease is not yet available, and when all the relevant information on the causes of abnormal drinking has been gathered in, the decision as to alcoholism being a disease will still rest very much on the definition of "alcoholism" on the one hand and "disease" on the other.[11]

He, thus, directs our attention to what we have already seen to be a crucial question for the sociologist, namely; the question of "what counts as" something for particular people in particular social situations, and what are the implications for social behaviour of those taken-for-granted definitions. For the sociologist is a non-starter in the race to define "alcoholism" and "alcoholic" so that such definitions can be universally applied to indicate diseases to be consulted about, cured or studied, or people to be treated or helped, prosecuted, sympathized with or admired. He is not in the business to "take", in Seeley's terms,[12] the professional's problems. Although, of course, he may certainly attempt to offer an explanation of why the professional sees what he sees *as* a problem. The professional's problem then becomes problematic for the sociologist.

But despite the professional's difficulty and debate over the

construction of universally acceptable definitions, it is nevertheless the case that people (both professional and lay) do
employ the notions "alcoholism" and "alcoholic" in respect of
what are for them, at that time, clearly delineated classes of
states and persons. Further, their action is informed by these
definitions and by their assumptions concerning the definitions
of significant others. It is thus, with the mundane use of such
notions as "alcoholism" and "alcoholic" and with the criteria
for, and implications of, such characterizations in particular
settings that the sociologist will be concerned.

However, this chapter is entitled "becoming ill". Thus, we
are asking not only "how do people define particular illness
conditions?" but also "how do they come to occupy the social
position of sick person or patient?" We saw in the previous
chapter that to say that someone occupies a social position
means that they share a certain social characteristic with other
people. In addition, because they occupy that particular social
position they and other people have certain expectations about
the way they ought to behave. Although we might all disagree
on points of detail in respect of particular people or particular
illness conditions most people tend to operate with the notion
that "a patient" has certain *rights* such as freedom from
particular normal obligations and certain *duties* such as co-
operating with professional medical personnel and making an
effort to get well again as speedily as possible. In addition, of
course, certain requirements are imposed upon the family,
friends, or work mates of the patient. These people may be
expected to put themselves out to a certain extent in order to
care for the patient, or in some way to ease the period of his
illness, and aid his recovery and the resumption of his normal
business of life.

Clearly, then, there are two major related strands which
must run through any consideration of how a person becomes
ill. One deals with differential exposure to illness conditions,
while the other concentrates upon differential perceptions of
and responses to those conditions.

Differential exposure to illness conditions

Man's social and physical environment determines to a certain degree the way in which he lives, and this is intimately bound up with his exposure and susceptibility to disease conditions. His pattern of life, the work which he does, the place in which he lives, and the recreation which he pursues may all increase or decrease the likelihood of his contracting particular diseases, and may encourage or impede their development.

That some diseases are associated with specific occupations, as pneumoconiosis is with mining, is a common-place. It is the epidemiologist's task to study the occurrence and distribution of diseases in a population. His skills are particularly useful where there is widespread agreement about what is to count as a particular disease or illness condition. Cholera, smallpox, T.B. and measles would all fall into such a category. In such cases the question of distribution can assume a key importance. However, the epidemiologist is not today merely concerned with contagious diseases, but also with chronic disease and disability. His approach, moreover, is not limited to physical health but is employed also in the study of mental illness, suicide, accidents, and other phenomena whose definition is much more open to debate both within the profession and without. By determining the scope and distribution of disease, once defined, it is the epidemiologist's task then to identify the particular foci of disease as they are related to subgroups of the population. Some diseases may be found among the poor, others among the rich, some among women, others among men, some among the young, others among the old, some among the married, others among the single, some among those with a particular occupation, others among those who live in a particular locality, and so on.

Once the epidemiologist has identified a pattern of disease his task is to construct some logical explanation for why the pattern is as it is. The mere identification of a pattern of disease may be a vital administrative device for indicating groups who would benefit from the special provision of preventive measures or therapeutic procedures. But however valuable this may be for making more bearable the lives of that particular section of the population the epidemiologist must attempt to identify factors related to disease causation. Coe[13] outlines a classic example of the epidemiologic method which is well worth repeating here.

> In 1855, there occurred in London a terrible outbreak of cholera which had caused over 500 deaths in less than ten days. At the time Sir John Snow attempted to identify the source of the epidemic in an effort to stop it. In pouring over the lists of deceased and afflicted persons while looking for common factors, he noted that the epidemic was most severe in a particular part of London and although cases of cholera had been reported in several areas, the majority of them had occurred in the neighbourhood of Broad Street. Upon interviewing members of the families of the deceased, Snow was able to isolate a single common factor, namely the Broad Street pump, from which victims had drunk in every case. Corroborating evidence was made from the observation that in the local workhouse, also in the Broad Street area, only a few inmates had contracted cholera and that in every case they had contracted it before being admitted to the workhouse. Snow hypothesised (and found) that the workhouse drew water from a separate well. Similar findings were made in other establishments. The pay off for Snow's careful investigation occurred when, finally convinced that impure water from the Broad Street pump was the cause of the cholera, Snow appealed to the authorities to have the pump closed. What makes this investigation unusual is the fact that the cholera bacillus was not discovered, by Robert Koch, until some twenty-eight years after Snow's investigation. Thus, even though Snow did not know the precise cause of cholera, by following a logical sequence of steps he was able to isolate and identify the source of the infection and to prescribe ways of combating it.

Despite the spectacular advances in medical science there is much that remains unknown, particularly about chronic, degenerative and non-communicable diseases. A major problem is that many of the most common present day illness conditions are not caused by a single readily identifiable agent, but seem rather to be the product of the interaction of several factors.

Since this is the case it is necessary to look for causes beyond the specific individual with a disease or illness condition to the habits, customs, and interaction patterns of particular social groups. However, before we leave the traditional epidemiologist it would be wise to consider one of his major tools: the health survey. For a detailed discussion of the various uses and methods of epidemiology other books must be consulted.[14]

Health surveys

One way of identifying patterns of disease, once the question of definition is acceptably solved, is to conduct a health survey. Such surveys are often used in order to answer questions about the prevalence (the total number of cases, at any *point* in time) and incidence (the total number of *new* cases in any *period* of time) of a particular illness condition in a particular population. At first sight such an exercise might appear to be fairly straightforward. There are, however, severe difficulties for those who attempt *any* kind of survey.

The first problem arises when there is the necessity to sample the population under investigation. Although it would be nice to be able to contact everyone within the study population this is usually out of the question. Such a procedure would usually be either too costly or too time consuming. But, whatever the size of the sample we eventually decide upon, the key question which must inform our construction of it is "what population am I hoping to make general statements about on the basis of material collected in the survey?" The following example concerning cancer will illustrate some of the problems facing those who wish to use health surveys. The example will also, and most importantly, indicate the kind of questions which we need to be satisfied about when reading the reports of health surveys conducted by other people.

Let us assume that, for whatever reason, we wish to determine the prevalence of breast cancer in London. Let us assume, further, that we have been commissioned to conduct a survey to provide an answer to this question, and that we have enough time and money to interview 10,000 people. We now have two fundamental problems. Which 10,000 people shall we interview, and what shall we ask them once we do interview them?

As to the first problem, we could go out into Oxford Street and ask the first 10,000 passers-by to give us their estimation of the number of people in London with breast cancer. We could then average out these estimates and come up with an "answer" to our problem. Clearly this will be unsatisfactory. A more realistic method might be to employ 100 interviewers, each of whom would go on a particular day to a doctor's surgery or hospital in the London area and ask 100 patients whether or not they were there because they had cancer of the breast. This would certainly be an improvement on the first method. However, it would only tell us about those cases of breast cancer which had already been identified. Similarly, it would only tell us about people who were consulting their doctor on that particular day. We would also miss those people who lived in London and were consulting a doctor outside London, and would we want to include in the number those people in hospitals and doctor's waiting-rooms who did not live in London? What would we count as London anyway? Would it be living in the G.L.C. area, or working in the G.L.C. area, or both, or having a doctor in the G.L.C. area, or what? Clearly we would not be much more satisfied with the second method of investigation that we were with the first. A third way to approach the problem would be to make a thorough study of all medical records in all hospitals and general practices to see how many cases of cancer of the breast were mentioned. A difficulty with such a method is that very few practices keep systematic and up-to-date records. The main drawback is, of course, that these records would only tell us about *identified* cases of breast cancer which had been *consulted about*.

The only really satisfactory way of answering the question about the prevalence of breast cancer in London is to take our sample of 10,000 from the general population of London. We must then discover how many of these 10,000 have breast cancer and extrapolate that proportion to the population of London as a whole to enable us to answer the question "what the prevalence of breast cancer is for that area?" Again, however, it is necessary to make a decision about which 10,000 people we shall have in our sample in order that we have a representative clinical and social picture of London as a whole.

Since breast cancer is so very rare in males it would be perfectly reasonable to consider only the female population of London for our study. But what characteristics would we expect those women to possess? Perhaps we should include women of each age group from twelve to 100, or women from each London borough. One major problem here, of course, is that there are no "lists of all the women in London" from which such samples could be drawn. Electoral rolls are always out of date and only include those who choose to be included. In addition, such a list would only include women over voting age. An attempt to draw a sample from doctors' practice lists would be similarly unsatisfactory since lists can never be complete or up to date and again include only those who have chosen to register with a doctor.

It is obviously easy to raise all sorts of objections to particular sampling strategies. But the fundamental point to keep fixed in our minds is that the nature of the sample determines the status of the statements which can be made at the end of the study about the population as a whole. Merely asking the first 10,000 women we meet in London if they have breast cancer will in no way enable us to estimate the prevalence of breast cancer in that city. In order that something valid can be said about London women as a whole from the sample of 10,000 we must be sure, and able to demonstrate to those who will read and take note of our report, that the sample is as *representative* of the total population as possible.

To be representative the sample must reflect as many variables relevant to the question under discussion as possible. At a common-sense level we would probably want the sample to contain the same age distribution as the female population as a whole, and the same social class distribution. In addition, we would probably want it to be representative as to geographical spread, marital status, family size, and medical history. These are all variables which from the outset we might expect to be related to breast cancer and therefore must be proportionally represented in our sample. Clearly, the sample cannot be representative in every dimension. Hair colour, foot size, astrological sign, car ownership and pet possession, for example, would in all probability be ignored as *defining* variables for the sample.

Let us now assume that somehow we manage to complete a list of the names and addresses of 10,000 people who we consider to be a representative sample of the population of London. What do we do with them? Since the aim of the survey is to discover the prevalence of breast cancer it will be insufficient merely to sign up a team of sociologists or market research interviewers, approach these people, and inquire from them whether or not they have this condition. Clearly the 10,000 will have to be examined by medically qualified persons who can answer this question for us. This, however, raises a further difficulty since such an examination would require the voluntary co-operation of the 10,000 subjects.

Some women would refuse to take part in the survey and decisions would have to be made about what should be done with their refusals. Should these people be ignored? Should we just concentrate on finding the proportion of the remaining members of the sample who have breast cancer? The answer is probably that the refusals should not be ignored if they account for more than a very small proportion of the total sample. If for instance only 1 per cent of the sample refuse and we discover that 14 per cent of the remainder have breast cancer then we can say that we assume that between 14 per cent and 15 per cent of the population of London have this condition. For most purposes that would be perfectly acceptable. But what if 30 per cent of the sample refused to participate? It would probably not then be very helpful to say that between 14 per cent and 44 per cent of the female population of London had breast cancer.

If 30 per cent of our sample did refuse to submit to a medical examination we could only ignore them if we can confidently assume that their refusal was in no way related to either the object of the survey or to any of the defining dimensions upon which the sample was constructed. In short, we can only ignore the refusals if we are pretty certain that the women who refused did so merely because they don't like taking part in social surveys and if in addition they are representative of the sample as a whole and not over representative of women of, for example, a particular age, race, or class category.

However, if we suspect that some of these women refused because they did not want to have a medical examination, or because they feared that they had cancer then they cannot be ignored. If there are a large number of such refusals then the whole study may have to be declared invalid. That is, the sample may be so depleted that we no longer have confidence that it is representative of the larger population from which it was drawn. Consequently, in our breast cancer example, any data on the proportion of a very depleted sample with the condition could not be usefully generalized to the population of London as a whole.

The "clinical iceberg"

One of the criticisms which was raised in connection with surveying hospital patients and patients in general practice waiting-rooms in connection with our hypothetical cancer study was that such an approach would reveal only reported and diagnosed instances of the condition under discussion. Various field studies in recent years have shown how unrepresentative are the samples drawn from such medical contexts.

Although there is a grudging recognition that each of us will die sometime, illness is often assumed by the general public to be a relatively infrequent, unusual or abnormal phenomenon.

Moreover, the statistics used in the discussion of illness tend to support this assumption. Specifically diagnosed conditions, days out of work, hospitalization, and consultations with a doctor do occur for most people relatively infrequently. Although such information only deals with professionally validated illness few people question whether it gives an adequate picture of the situation. Usually implicit also is the notion that people who do not consult their doctor or some other professional agency, and thus do not appear in official medical statistics, may be regarded as healthy. Since the advent of periodic health surveys, however, widespread notice has had to be taken of what the medical profession has always known, namely, that for many conditions the cases which are presented for diagnosis and treatment merely constitute the tip of "the clinical iceberg".

Health surveys have noted that as much as 90 per cent of their apparently healthy subjects had some physical aberration or clinical disorder well worthy of treatment.[15] Moreover, neither the type of the disorder nor its severity, by medical standards, differentiated those who felt ill from those who did not. In the pioneering Peckham Study,[16] even of those who felt ill only 40 per cent were under medical care.

Such data as these have caused many to question some of their ideas about illness. Instead of being a relatively infrequent unusual phenomenon the empirical reality seems to be that the presence of clinically serious symptoms is the statistical norm. To make the situation absolutely plain, Hinkle and associates[17] noted that the average lower middle class American male experiences between the ages of twenty and forty approximately one life endangering episode, twenty disabling illnesses, 200 non-disabling illnesses and 1,000 symptomatic episodes. That is, on average, one new episode every six days.

The frequent occurrence of particular illness symptoms in untreated apparently healthy populations must mean one of two things. If the symptom is believed to have medical significance when observed in a medical setting then either the attribution of significance is unwarranted or there are many people going about their business who require medical attention but are not receiving it. This leads us to the second main concern of this chapter. That is, from a consideration of differential exposure to illness conditions to a consideration of the differential perception of and responses to them.

Differential responses to illness conditions

Just as people, because of the way they choose or are required to live, may be differentially exposed to illness conditions so they may differ in other ways. First they may differ in their readiness to interpret a particular sign as a symptom of illness. Second, they may differ in their readiness to consult about or seek help for any particular symptoms of illness which they perceive. Questions of the meaning of illness episodes for those involved are closely linked with the causation of disease, with wider social problems, and with administrative and economic considerations relating to the provision of medical care.

Suchman[18] stresses the multi-causality of illness conditions and the importance of a consideration of the socio-environmental context when he writes that

> there is a complex interplay between socio-environmental factors, social problems, health conditions, and public health programmes. Each one may lead to the other in a myriad of different ways. On the one hand socio-environmental factors may result in physical conditions conducive to ill health. These unhealthy conditions may in turn be defined as social problems if the community becomes concerned and seeks to remove them. For example, poor housing (a physical condition) may lead to the growth of slums (a social problem) which in turn increases exposure to tuberculosis (a health condition), which then requires the development of preventive and therapeutic measures (a public health program). On the other hand, certain public health problems such as venereal disease, become social problems as they impinge upon the value structure of the community.

There is an intimate relationship, therefore, between questions of health and illness and the values and priorities of a particular society, social group or individual. Thus, it is essential to consider what health and illness *mean* to the people involved in any illness situation and what are the implications for themselves or others of "being ill" and occupying the social position of patient. Only by attempting to understand what such things mean to the people involved can we say why "a person" becomes "a patient" and why one person with a particular illness condition consults about it when another person with apparently the same condition does not.

Everyone has some idea of what it means to be a patient. That is, we all have certain expectations about the way we expect people to behave who occupy the social position of patient. If this is the case then whether or not people consult about the symptoms they perceive is likely to be influenced by how they evaluate the effect which "being a patient", and performing the patient role as they define it, will have upon the normal business of their life. In some cases, for example when a person is injured in a road accident, the potential patient has little choice about whether he will be placed under medical care and become "a hospital patient". In the vast majority of illness episodes, however, the options are much more open, both for the symptomatic person and for those about him. Mrs M's account of her husband's leg injury in a study of the process of becoming ill[19] illustrates the kind of manoeuvrings which can be made around the notion of being ill, and also around the idea of the appropriate role of the doctor.

Mr M., aged 28, twisted his knee playing football on the Saturday prior to the Wednesday upon which Mrs M. spoke of the episode. She reported that her husband had not consulted their doctor even though the pain had gradually become worse and by the Wednesday was preventing him from driving their old car.

Mrs M. said, "It wasn't too bad when he came in, just tender round the knee. It was stiff (on) Sunday and I said he'd have to go to the surgery on Monday . . . but he wouldn't. He started his new job with X's and you can't go sick on the first day. He'd have got his note no trouble last month. Last week he was home anyway (between jobs) I could have looked after him. Just rest and he wouldn't have needed the doctor. Trust him to do it when he can't be on the sick. Next week he can make out he did it on site. It's not that bad mind.*

It can be seen from this short statement that Mrs M. had quite clear ideas about when it was appropriate for Mr M. to "go sick" and when to consult the doctor. Furthermore, these ideas about appropriate behaviour were largely independent of the seriousness of the injury condition. They were bound up rather with a consideration of other commitments with which Mr M. was faced.

When Mr M. had (the previous month) been with his old employer as a laundry-delivery-van driver it would have been quite in order for him to have taken time off work in order to consult his doctor and get the necessary medical certificate to legitimize a period of sick leave. During the time between jobs Mrs M. could have looked after her husband and, because rest was all that Mr M. was (falsely) considered to require, he "wouldn't have needed the doctor". However, Mr and Mrs M. felt that the demands and obligations of being in his new job as a machine operator were such that it was impossible, even though the condition was worsening, to take time off to go to the doctor and thus run the risk of being "on the sick".

Because of the M. family's perception of the seriousness of the injury (false as it turned out), the doctor was not initially considered in terms of his capacity as healer but solely in terms of his capacity as agent of legitimation for access to the social position of patient. That is, Mrs M. spoke of him only as a

* In fact when Mr M. did go to the doctor the following week, and subsequently to the out-patient department, it was revealed that ligaments in his knee were damaged. He was off work for over two months and the injury almost certainly put a premature end to his football playing.

provider of sick notes and not as a provider of medical care.
The doctor's role as healer was only thought to be relevant
when the injury was subsequently felt to be in need of specialist
medical treatment.

This short example highlights the importance of a consideration of the meaning and common-sense definition and interpretation of illness episodes for the particular people involved.
Clearly, illness can not be thought of as an independent
isolated issue either for the symptomatic person or for those
around him. In fact, behaviour in illness situations can only
be understood by placing the illness episode in its social context
and evaluating the meaning of the situation for the participants
in terms of their perception of the benefits and drawbacks of
particular courses of action. A person who arrives at a doctor's
surgery or at a hospital out-patient department does so after a
whole series of prior decisions. One of the tasks of medical
sociology is to set out the implications of the fact that people
differ systematically, according to their values, beliefs and
basic conditions of life, in their ideas about which signs can
legitimately be classified as symptoms of what illness in which
people, when, and what should be done about them.

It was mentioned earlier that people are frequently called
upon to make decisions about illness conditions and responses
to them. But what does it mean to talk about decision-making
in illness situations? "Decision-making" says Selznick[20] "is one
of those fashionable phrases that may well assume more that it
illuminates". Clearly, it is a phrase to be careful about.
Decisions, however, are what we continually infer have been
made. We often assume that since person X follows course of
action Y he has carefully weighted up the alternatives and
"decided" that course of action Y does suit his needs best.
Since this is what we, as actors, actually assume in social
situations sociologists must understand these assumptions and
analyse particular situations accordingly.

In any illness situation a whole series of decisions *can* be made
by particular categories of person. Whether any of them *are*
made depends upon how the actors in the situation interpret

the facts of their social life. One feature of illness episodes which encourages both sociologists and participants to think in terms of decision-making is that it is difficult for the actor to ignore them. As long as symptoms last he is likely to consider them. He may, as doctor, or potential patient, or member of the potential patient's family, take no action but he cannot easily withdraw from the situation.

In the previously mentioned study of the process of becoming ill[21] each family filled out a health diary for a period of a month. Each day every perceived symptom was noted for each member of the family, together with a report of any action taken and any other comments about the episode which the wife-mother felt like making. An episode reported in one of these health diaries will illustrate a series of considerations and "decisions" made in response to the mother's perception of one minor illness symptom. Andrew (Mrs N's three-and-a-half-year-old son) wet himself several times one day. Mrs N. reported this in the diary and since Andrew had been "dry" for some time considered it worthy of note as a potential illness symptom.

Throughout the episode, from the initial perception of the symptom on day one to a fortnight later when Mrs N. reported that she would not "go to doctor yet" the situation was continually being assessed and re-assessed. When the symptom was first perceived it was categorized as noteworthy but not serious. The explanation was offered that Andrew, since he had just begun to go out by himself to play with other children, was too pre-occupied to bother about the fact that he was wetting his trousers. However, on day two the situation changed. Andrew wet his bed during the night, thereby casting doubt on Mrs N's explanation for the previous day's occurrences. In addition Andrew was complaining of a burning sensation "when passing water". In response to this and the fact that Mrs N. noticed a "strong smell of ammonia with his sheets" the only piece of positive action taken during the fortnight was initiated – Andrew was given more water to drink, while his sugar intake was cut down. After this there was some improvement.

On day three, Andrew only "complained a little" when passing water and had been "dry" during the previous night. On day four the only comments were those indicating that there was nothing adverse to comment about – "no complaining from Andrew today and dry again last night". Clearly, although the child was not exhibiting any symptoms the episode was not over for Mrs N. She was still aware of the possibility that he might be ill or becoming ill and was concerned to note even the absence of symptoms. On days five and six Mrs N. noted the "very unusual" fact that Andrew woke up in the night to pass water. However, when pressed on this point Mrs N. was ready to acknowledge that, in fact, this was not a very unusual occurrence at all. Because she was so concerned about noticing whenever her son passed or did not pass water she became sensitive to the slightest change in usual behaviour.

After the episode she spoke of always "wondering what to do really for the best" because, as she added, "what was all right to do yesterday may be wrong today, that's the difficulty I find". Although the only real action which Mrs N. had taken in response to Andrew's condition was to increase his water intake and cut down his sugar on day two she was quite aware herself, as the diary showed, of how much time she spent weighing up and re-assessing the situation. Once the symptom had been perceived she could not ignore it. She had continually to be seeking for evidence and "making decisions".

On day seven Andrew again wet his cot. In spite of all the discussion and observations by Mrs N. this was only the second time this had happened in the whole episode. But the fact that it had happened more than once set Mrs N. "wondering if this is just a temporary lapse" since he had been "dry for at least eighteen months". Again, however, when Mrs N. was questioned about this later she did admit that Andrew had occasionally wet his bed in the eighteen months during which he was supposed to have been "dry". On day seven this had been forgotten in her concern about whether or not the present episode was "just a temporary lapse". On days eight, nine and ten nothing happened. Then on days eleven and twelve Andrew wet his cot again. Clearly Mrs N. was forced to conclude that this may not be just "a temporary lapse" so she mentioned the possibility of seeing the doctor the following week. Even at this stage, though, after twelve days Mrs N. was not willing definitely to consult her G.P. She put in the scale against consulting the fact that Andrew was "perfectly happy" and that "there is no recurrence of burning". She again decided to just wait and see. By day fifteen after three clear days she was able to write that there was no need to "go to the doctor yet". The diary month finished four days after this entry so there was little opportunity for further details in this episode. In fact the episode was over as far as Mrs N. was concerned and Andrew was "dry" again.

The classification of symptoms and defining of behaviour as either relevant or not relevant for reporting to professional medical authorities is a fact of everyday life for most families. In the case of Andrew and his bed-wetting very little action was taken and in the end the doctor was not consulted. Andrew did not end up in any official medical statistics, but could very well have done if he had wet his bed just once more on day thirteen, or if he had complained of "burning" on one of the later days. In itself one more wet bed is of no great importance but to Mrs N., since she was sensitive to the possibility of consulting a doctor, it may just have been the final trigger needed to send her to the surgery. Since she had perceived the symptom it was impossible for her to ignore it.

Particular people in particular social situations will be presented with the opportunity for making illness-related decisions in which they recognize the necessity to evaluate at least two courses of action – whether to do something or to do nothing. It is the medical sociologist's task to attempt an interpretive understanding of subsequent action by taking account of the assumed decision-making process. From an analysis of the family data it became apparent that a series of clear cut, overt decisions, such as those exemplified by the case of Mr M's twisted knee, were rare. Neither were there many long-drawn out series of assessments as in the case of Andrew's bed-wetting. For the most part the principal actors in any illness situation did not consider more than one course of action. There was no thinking-out and weighing-up of alternative strategies to obtain a series of defined goals when, for example, mothers put antiseptic cream on grazed knees, took aspirin for a headache, kept children in the house when they had chills, or called in the doctor when someone's temperature was found to be 102°. These mothers knew what to do and did it.

However, this is not to say, of course, that confronted with the same physical indications they would all have done the *same* thing. But in what sense is this "knowing what to do and doing it" decision-making? There is no sense, in such cases, in which evidence is assessed and one course of action taken rather than another in the light of an evaluation of that evidence. However, this is not to say that the seemingly unconsidered action is not rational. Someone may hold a belief without continually assessing evidence and drawing conclusions. "It is enough", says Gibson[22] "that either all at once by systematic enquiry or gradually through trial error" a person "has found out that certain things are necessary, or sufficient, if certain things are to follow".

The mother does not necessarily weigh up the value of keeping her child indoors when he has a sore throat against taking him to the doctor, against doing nothing at all, or against giving the child some cough mixture. The "decision" may be made by reference to time past or from the example of others, or at the suggestion of her mother, or from remembrance of her own treatment in a similar case, or from her recent reading of a magazine article reporting on the outbreak of sore throats among young children.

Since symptomatic episodes occur regularly their course can be observed and their treatment explored. People acquire a body of knowledge about them. This body of knowledge might be called magic belief in one community, folk medicine in another and medical science in a third. Nevertheless, at whatever level it is likely to include some kind of classification of episodes, evaluation of the nature and significance of common symptoms, and predictions relating to the probable outcome of illnesses and their usual handling. It is with reference to this body of knowledge that most illness decisions are made.

Although a separate chapter is devoted to "Medicine: a Particular Profession", it is essential to remind ourselves that it is unhelpful to make a rigid division between, on the one hand, a consideration of the patient or potential patient and, on the other, consideration of the doctor. The interaction *between* the doctor and the patient is something in which the sociologist is keenly interested and an understanding of which has obvious implications for the satisfactory provision of medical care and the administration of medical services.

When people seek medical care, and thus engage in the process of "becoming a patient", their progress can be visualized as moving between two interrelated sets of demands, actions, values and social interactions: between one, the everyday life of the patient, and the other, the professional therapeutic system of organized medicine. However, people seeking professional care for some perceived symptom or illness condition and those from whom they seek it may have divergent and, at times, conflicting interests and priorities. Some patients may be more concerned with primary symptoms, pain and social incapacitation than with underlying organic diseases. They may be oriented towards a speedy return to normal or satisfactory minimum social functioning rather than complete physiological health. Members of the medical profession, on the other hand, may concentrate more on clinical illness than on the physical discomforts of its symptoms or its social consequences. These difference of orientation, goals and definition of what is of primary importance may lead to conflict between the patient and his doctor.

Once these points are taken certain implications follow for medical practice and administration. An interview with any experienced medical practitioner will reveal that he does not, and knows he does not, operate with a simple model of illness, which implies that through a history, physical examination and evaluation of laboratory reports he can justify, find an

objective account for, or explain, the particular complaint
presented to him. However, the realization that certain extra-
medical factors are involved in the development and presentation of many complaints often goes no further than an attempt
to explain some behaviour in illness situations, which can not
be understood as a straight response to recognizable disorders,
by the use of such blanket terms as psychosomatic illness,
hypochondria, malingering and the like. These terms often
serve merely to define the episode out of the practitioner's
court.

One of the aims of this book is to show that such a response
is neither satisfactory nor all that is possible. The sociologist's
attempt to point up certain similarities between social categories of patients and potential patients and to highlight
certain constellations of ideas about appropriate behaviour for
particular people in illness situations has clear implications for
medical practice which might not otherwise be gained from the
perspective of the clinician whose primary concern is likely to
be with individual aberrations.

Thus, if we are to understand peoples' action in relation to
questions of health and illness, such actions must always be
considered in conjunction with assessment of current ideas,
demands and beliefs about appropriate ways of behaving. If,
as health surveys have demonstrated, treated illness is only a
portion of existing symptoms and pathology, and if the decision
to seek aid is based at least as much on social circumstances as
biological-physiological ones then studies of the causation of
disorders based upon treated population must be studied with
caution. For example,[23] it was formerly believed that Buerger's
disease was particularly prevalent among East European Jews.
Later it was discovered that this "medical fact" was due not
so much to the nature of either the disease or East European
Jews as to the fact that Dr Buerger made his observations at
Mount Sinai hospital. This lighthearted example illustrates the
price of ignoring patterns of illness behaviour. But what of more
important examples?

The massively comprehensive and detailed *Atlas of Disease*

Mortality[24] sets out spacial patterns of variations in disease mortality in England and Wales. It states that "the aim of the atlas is not to suggest associations between certain areas and certain diseases but rather to provide the factual material upon which future work may be based. The maps should provide a useful pattern to the areas with unfavourable mortality experience in which detailed research might profitably be initiated."

That is a very fair statement about, and warning to the users of, the Atlas. However, it is to be hoped, when research is initiated in particular areas that consideration of illness behaviour will not be ignored. It is a large jump from Mr M's twisted knee to the *National Atlas of Disease Mortality*. But the M. family made a series of considered decisions about "becoming a patient" in the light of other social demands. It is, therefore, likely that similar series of decisions will affect people's readiness to consult about symptoms which may eventually turn out to be indicators of disease which would result in those people adding to the numbers in the National Atlas. It is not inconceivable that a persistent sore throat may be tolerated by the vast majority of Luton car workers more than by school teachers for whom it would be an impediment to the performance of one of their major social roles. This is a simple example, but indicative of the kind of question which could be asked by those whose job it is to interpret the "factual material" of the National Atlas, or hospital records, or differential consulting rates, or prescribing patterns in general practice, or any other data relating to the provision or administration of medical care.

This chapter has stressed that if we are to understand the way in which people behave in illness situations and thus are to be able to make adequate predictions about the use of medical facilities and the nature of illness conditions which are presented to professional medical agencies we must concern ourselves with the meaning of illness situations for the actors involved. For notions such as physical and mental illness have no absolute meaning. These concepts only have relevance when we specify the particular demands that persons must cope with and the life they must or wish to live. When these demands and ideas about life change then health services, if they are to remain at all effective, must recognize them and change accordingly in terms of their own demands and aims. As Dubos[25] in "Mirage of Health" so elegantly puts it:

> Health is not a state of being it is a process of adaptation to the changing demands of living and the changing meanings we give to life itself.

It is against this background that any consideration of how "a person" becomes "a patient" must be made.

Summary

The aim of this chapter has been to show that the sociologist's concern with illness is not merely a concern with illness conditions. The distinction was stressed at the outset between the possession of some symptom or illness condition and concomitant behaviour. The distinction was between diseases, illness conditions, disability, symptoms, disorder, on the one hand, and "being ill", on the other. In short, the study of illness behaviour is the study of the social concomitants of illness conditions and the relation of one to the other.

An attempt was made to indicate the nature of the sociologist's contribution to the explanation of medical problems. The medical sociologist was seen to be concerned, among other things, to delineate "what counts" for particular people in particular situations *as* an illness condition. The examples of obesity, breast cancer and alcoholism were mentioned. Since people's actions are informed by their definitions of illness and by their assumptions concerning the definitions of significant others, the sociologist's task is to set out the criteria for and implications of such characterizations of illness in particular situations. But, as has been stressed, a consideration of "becoming ill" involves not only a concern with how people define, are exposed to, or come to possess or be seen to have illness conditions, but also a concern with how people come to occupy the social position of sick person or patient.

In a discussion of differential exposure to illness conditions the epidemiologic method was briefly discussed and certain problems associated with the notion of "the clinical iceberg" and the conducting of health surveys were indicated. Examples from a study of the process of becoming ill showed the classification of symptoms as either relevant or not relevant for presentation to medical authorities, and the separate but intimately related question of the symptomatic person as either occupying or not occupying legitimately the social position of patient, to be constant facts of everyday life for most families. In sum, the chapter stressed that if we are to understand the way in which people behave in illness situations and thus are to be able to make realistic predictions about the use of and need for medical facilities, and about the nature of those illness conditions which will or will not be presented to particular medical agencies, it is necessary to gain some understanding of the meaning of particular illness situations for all those involved.

Suggestions for further reading:

Apple, D. How Laymen Define Illness. *J. Health & Human Behaviour*, *1*, *219*, 1960.

Mechanic, D. The Concept of Illness Behaviour. *J.Chron.Dis.*, *15*, *189*, 1961.

Morris, J.N. *Uses of Epidemiology*. 2nd Ed., E. & S. Livingstone, Edinburgh and London, 1964.

Robinson, D. *The Process of Becoming Ill*. Routledge & Kegan Paul, London, 1971.

Zola, I.K. Culture and Symptoms: an analysis of patients' presenting complaints. *American Sociological Review*, *XXXI*, 615, 1966.

CHAPTER III

The Patient: a Social Position

"With the starting of an illness a number of secondary processes are also set in motion. One may say that the illness creates a new life-situation to which the patient must adapt himself."

Balint[1]

The previous chapter pointed to the close interrelationship between the social and the biological criteria for defining someone as ill. The example of Mr M. and his twisted knee demonstrated how the definition of "being ill" was intimately bound up with a consideration of the meaning of the particular symptom, and its consequences, for the symptomatic person and significant others. The seriousness of the illness and the liklihood of consulting professional medical agencies was not determined solely by reference to such questions as the amount of pain or discomfort being suffered or the degree of physical impairment, but was determined also by the way in which these things were related to and given meaning by the particular social context in which the episode occurred. The process of becoming ill was, thus, seen to be a bio-social process.

By entitling this chapter "The Patient: a Social Position" attention is being refocused upon the crucial distinction between the possession of symptoms or illness conditions and the possible socially relevant consequences of those symptoms or conditions. The distinction is between such things as disease, illness condition, symptom and disorder on the one hand and "being ill" on the other; between conditions and social action. The medical sociologist's concern is with the social action concomitants of illness conditions and with the relationship between the two. Mechanic,[2] we remember, labelled this concern "the study of illness behaviour", which he defined as "the way in which given symptoms may be differentially perceived, evaluated, and acted (or not acted) upon by different kinds of person".

In the previous chapter it was seen how the apparently simple question "how many people in London have breast cancer?" was difficult to answer even with the aid of health survey techniques. The difficulties over definition, sampling, and reporting were quickly identified. Let us stay with the breast cancer example.

In the course of our health survey research it is reasonable to expect that a number of women would be found, as a result of the medical examination which was part of our study, to have cancer of the breast. Some of those women may have suspected their condition but not spoken of it or reported it to anyone else. For others, however, the fact of their cancer would be a revelation to them, to their doctor and to everyone else. As a result of the discovery some of these women would take whatever steps were suggested by professional medical authorities to undergo whatever treatment was felt to be desirable. On the other hand, it is quite likely that some women, after having the fact of their cancer given to them, would not agree to undergo any treatment, and would not agree to the information being divulged to either their family doctor or to members of their family.

In respect of all these women it is quite legitimate to ask, and very difficult to answer, the common-sense question "when did they become ill?" Was it when the cancer developed, or when it was discovered in the health survey, or when the symptomatic person was informed by the survey doctor, or when the treatment was initiated, or when the "fact" of the cancer was made public to the family doctor and to members of the family, or when? Such questions clearly illustrate the difficulties over definition which are encountered when the distinction is not maintained between, on the one hand, having a disease and, on the other, being a sick person or patient. The difficulty stems from the fact that both things; the possession of an illness condition, known or not, and the occupancy of a social position, can be subsumed under the one heading of "being ill".

A person occupies a social position and performs the role consistent with it only when one or more significant others identify and treat them as someone legitimately occupying that position. Any study of patients, therefore, must concern itself with the criteria with which people operate to define someone as legitimately occupying the social position of patient. To claim to be a "sick person" or "patient" is not a sufficient condition of definition. Some writers distinguish between the sick-role and the patient-role.[3] However, such a distinction, which rests usually upon the rather too rigid adherence to a prior distinction between professional and non-professional, official and unofficial, medical intervention, need not concern us here. Occupancy of the social position of sick-person or patient (we shall use them synonymously) may or may not be conditional, for particular people at particular times in particular situations, upon legitimacy by some professional medical agency. This, in fact, is one of the points at issue, to be found out and understood in particular illness situations and not to be definitionally decided at the outset. Therefore just as becoming a patient is seen to be a process of bargain and manoeuvre so being a patient, and performing the sick role, is a matter of mutual orientation as between the symptomatic person and significant others.

The notion of significant others has been mentioned previously and requires brief elucidation. It is core task of the sociologist to attempt to understand, explain, and point up implications for social action in particular situations, differing constructions of reality. In Chapter I it was emphasized that *social* action was, as Weber put it, action "oriented toward the past, present or expected behaviour of others", and that the "others" towards whom action is oriented may be known or unknown or may constitute an "indefinite plurality". Weber cited the exchange of money as an example of the latter possibility. Thus, of the symptomatic person in an illness situation, a particular concern of the medical sociologist, it will be possible to characterize all other people on the basis of whether or not they and their ideas are relevant to his action. In other words, it will be possible to say whether or not the symptomatic person's action is oriented by reference to them. The relevance of "others" is not determined by their occupancy of some social position in that particular illness situation, nor is it necessary that they should even be aware of it. Their importance stems from their relationship with the symptomatic person in some way, or setting, which *he* considers to be relevant to his action in the illness situation.

Among all relevant others the symptomatic person will distinguish some "significant others" with reference to whose real or presumed attitude he acts. This is *not* to say, however, that the symptomatic person will act in a way which is consistent with, or mutually acceptable to, those attitudes of the significant other(s), but merely that his action will be significantly informed by reference to them. Similarly, of course, the behaviour of *all* actors in the illness situation will be oriented to the behaviour of the symptomatic person and/or any other(s) significant for *them*.

But social action in particular illness situations should not be conceptualized as some kind of shadow boxing between individuals. For just as the symptomatic person's action will be informed by his interpretation of the actions and attitudes of particular significant others so it will also be informed by the habits, customs, doctrines and beliefs about what behaviour is appropriate in illness situations. Systems of beliefs about appropriate behaviour, normative systems, are to a greater or lesser extent shared. As such they are "facts" of the present which confront and constrain greater or lesser numbers of individuals. But however widespread a particular idea about appropriate behaviour may be there is ample opportunity for individuals and groups of individuals to disagree about, bargain over, and manoeuvre around, these bounds and constraints and around *actual* patterns of behaviour in particular situations. One of the key features of any analysis of action in relation to illness is, of course, the appropriate behaviour of the patient.

An understanding of ideas about the sick role is essential, therefore, if we are to describe or attempt to explain action in
illness situations.

The sick role

We all have certain ideas, though of course not exactly the
same ideas, about the way in which we expect a person to
behave who occupies the social position of sick person or
patient. We also have ideas about the appropriate way of
behaving towards someone who we consider is legitimately
classified as a patient. Although they have come in for a good
deal of close scrutiny[4] some of these ideas are helpfully
brought together in Talcott Parsons'[5] development of Sigerist's[6] formulation of the sick role. Four main aspects of the
sick role, as seen by Parsons, are that the sick person

1. Is exempt from certain normal social responsibilities
2. Cannot be expected to take care of himself or get rid of his
   illness by "willpower"
3. Should want to get well, and
4. Should seek medical advice and co-operate with medical
   experts.

As with the expectations concerning the occupancy of *any*
social position, "being a patient" is considered to involve certain
rights and certain duties. As Parsons puts it[7], there is "the
existence of a set of institutionalized expectations and the corre-
sponding sentiments and sanctions".

Exemption from normal social responsibilities

Exemption from certain normal social obligations is commonly accepted to be a major right of the sick person.[8] It is
essential to emphasize again here, however, that these "widely
accepted" notions are not fixed, or handed down on the tablets
of stone, but merely taken, in the light of research evidence
from wide varieties of societies and settings, to be recurrent
themes underpinning ideas about "being a patient". It is the

sociologist's task, as was indicated in Chapter I, to attempt to draw out common trans-situational themes, ideas, and patterns of behaviour from the everyday common-sense understandings in terms of which social action is oriented in particular situations.

It is suggested that we do not expect the patient to carry on *as normal* but to adapt his usual way of life by shedding some of his normal duties. These duties may be occupational, domestic, or recreational, but of whatever type they are put aside for the duration of the time that he is "a patient". Two related points need to be emphasized. First, the shedding of normal social responsibilities is not solely a right to be had on demand but has to be acceded to by relevant others. This legitimation might take the form of a sick note from a doctor or maybe merely a willingness on the part of other members of a family to cover for the sick person and temporarily to take over his duties. The second point to emphasize is that the putting aside of normal social duties can be a duty for the patient as well as a right. Just as the sick person may claim the right of avoiding obligations so others may demand that he avoids them even when he may not want to. It is not uncommon for someone to be told that they *ought* to stay at home from work with a particular condition. Here they are being encouraged to be a patient when they might really want to carry on with the normal business of their lives.

Clearly, in any situation the symptomatic person and/or significant others have ideas about the appropriateness of various courses of action. While the symptomatic person may be reluctant to adopt the sick role because the demands of other short-term obligations are too high, so significant others may encourage the symptomatic person to adopt the sick role because of the risks of long-term damage by not doing so. In the case of Mr M. and his twisted knee; if Mr and Mrs M. had realized the serious nature of the injury then Mr M. might have been willing to sacrifice the short-term social, economic, occupational gain of going to his new job on the first day, in order to benefit from the *long-term* physiological gain of seeking immediate specialist treatment, adopting the sick role and possibly being able to play football again when the knee had recovered.

In any situation, therefore, all those involved will have their own ideas about how ill the symptomatic person is and whether or not they can or should legitimately occupy the social position of patient. The question is seldom obvious and universally agreed upon but is usually ambiguous and open to competing interpretations. Which interpretation dominates for the symptomatic person and for significant others is a matter which can only be understood by taking into account the whole range of obligations and complex and competing demands which go to make up the social interaction in any illness situation.

The question of responsibility for the illness condition

The second major commonly accepted feature of "being a patient" is that one cannot be expected to get well by an act or decision of will. The patient is someone who has, as Parsons[9] puts it, "a condition that must be 'taken care of'. His 'condition' must be changed, not merely his 'attitude'. Of course, the process of recovery may be spontaneous but while the illness lasts he can't 'help it'." This notion of the patient being unable to help the condition is essential, but must be kept analytically separate from other closely related issues. The patient cannot be expected to mend a broken leg by willpower or get rid of pneumonia by sheer effort or determination or in response to an exortation to "try hard". The condition either has to right itself or be acted upon.

The patient cannot be blamed for having his condition, he is not "responsible" for it. However, he may have carelessly exposed himself to the possibility of getting the condition either by *doing* something such as driving recklessly or with too high an alcohol level in his blood, or *not doing* something, such as not being vaccinated against a particular disease. He may also act in a way which precludes help being given for the condition or which definitely makes the condition worse. But these points, absolutely vital as they are for our understanding of the cause, or outcome of an illness, or the reactions of others towards the symptomatic person, must be kept separate from the central point that the patient or sick person once he has contracted, gained, or succumbed to any particular illness condition can not get rid of it by willpower.

The way in which social action is seen, interpreted, and reacted to, both within and without illness situations is often based crucially upon the attribution of individual responsibility. We tend to distinguish between the legal and medical response to some deviation from perceived normality by saying that law deals with acts for which the individual is held to be accountable while medicine tends to deal with imputed deviance for which the individual is believed not responsible and is thus "treated" rather than "punished".

However, while this distinction holds by and large when illness is taken to refer to the disordered structure of the human body as a physical or biochemical machine it is more difficult to maintain when the attention of the medical profession becomes focused upon social disability or suffering or mental illness. One would like to be able to classify human problems in such a way that the therapeutic and legal/moral would emerge as exclusive alternatives. Then we could determine simply that any given issue calls for a medical rather than a legal response. The fear is often voiced, however, that the development of psychiatry has undermined altogether the possibility of moral and legal responsibility.[10] Thus, only a clear division between the moral and the therapeutic would seem to guarantee the security of our moral and legal traditions.

Some practices encourage us to look for such a division. For instance the famous M'naughten Rule (1843) for deciding legal insanity requires that it be

> Clearly proved that at the time of the act the accused was labouring under such a defect of reasoning as not to know the nature and quality of his act, or, if he did, that he did not know that what he was doing was wrong.[11]

We may be tempted to say that exemption under the M'naughten Rule serves to separate legal from medical cases so that an action is to be judged in legal terms or in medical terms but not in both. However, a moment's consideration is sufficient to reveal that the appeal to professional psychiatric opinion in itself is part of the *legal* procedure and contributes to a legal finding. A decision to treat rather than to punish in such a case is a legal decision. As Philip Roche remarks[12]

> In a strict sense the finding of insanity is not a medical function, it is a legal function even in civil matters. The psychiatrist is responsible only for the finding of mental illness by a medical criteria . . . it remains for some legal authority to pass upon such findings and to adjudicate insanity which is not a medical condition but an altered civil status which sets an individual apart from his fellows.

From this simple issue it can be seen that the contrast between the therapeutic psychiatric domain and the legal/moral domain lies not so much in the logical properties of the judgments rendered but rather in the practical handling of human beings whose actions are being judged. The crucial questions concern the sorting out of the responsibilities and the implications of attributing or denying responsibility. It is clear that the medical mode of response is being applied to more and more behaviours which have been responded to quite differently in the past. We may agree with Wootton[13] that ". . . in the contemporary attitude toward anti-social behaviour psychiatry and humanism have marched hand in hand . . .", that ". . . the medical treatment of social deviants has been a most powerful, perhaps even the most powerful, reinforcement of humanitarian impulses . . .", and that ". . . today the prestige of humane proposals is immensely enhanced if these are expressed in the idiom of medical science". But there are important implications for the layman and the professional in the tendency for the medical profession to impute illness where the layman sees something other than illness. While the professional may see "blindness" the layman may see "bad vision", where the professional sees "mental illness" the layman may see "nervousness" or "problems", and where the professional sees "alcoholism" the layman may see "heavy drinking". It is part of the sociologist's task to tease out these different perceptions and to attempt to explain their genesis and point up their implications.

It was noted in the last chapter that ideas about appropriate responses to particular behaviour may change over time. For example there has been widespread change in the nature of the response to excess drinking from that of considering it a moral failing to considering it a symptom of disease. However, by staying in the realm of "the addictions" we can see how responses to the consumption of various substances differ very strikingly. Let us consider substances such as heroin, tobacco, amphetamines, alcohol and cannabis, all of which could be expected to be mentioned in any contemporary discussion of "drug abuse".[14] Two complementary themes appear to lie at the heart of this commonly used notion. First is the excessive use of some substance which is freely available, second is the use, purchase, or possession, of some substance which is not freely available. In the first category, we have, in our society, such substances as alcohol and tobacco. The "abuse" in this case is the excessive use of a substance which is freely available for a large proportion of the population. The response to such "abuse" is usually medical. In the second category we have the mere use, as opposed to any idea of excessive use, of a substance by someone who is considered not entitled to use it at all. It may be the use of a substance, like heroin, which only a very small proportion of the population are entitled to use, or the use of a substance, like an amphetamine, without the authorization of a prescription from the medical profession, or the use of a freely available substance, like alcohol, but at the wrong age, or in the wrong place, or at the wrong time, or in the wrong company. The response to the second category of "abuse" is usually legal.

However, there are exceptions to both categories of response. In the case of excess use of a readily available substance a

person may find himself arrested for the offence of public
drunkenness, while in the case of an illegal substance a person
may find himself avoiding the legal consequences of being found
with heroin in his possession by being registered at a heroin
treatment clinic. But the medical response to this initially legal
offence is based upon the notion that certain people become
addicted to certain substances and are not able to resist alone
the need/desire to continue taking the substance. In other
words, they are deemed to have "lost control" in some sense,
and thus, by definition, can not be held entirely responsible
for their condition. We have come full circle then to our
initial consideration of the crucial notion of "not being able
to help" and "not being able to cure by willpower" which was,
as we noted earlier, one of the widely held notions underpinning the definition of "being a patient".

The desire to get well

The third commonly accepted component of the sick role
is that the person should want to get well as speedily as possible.
This is one of the obligations which the sick person is deemed
to have which justifies and counterbalances the rights which
he is afforded by virtue of his position as a patient. As Parsons[15]
says "the first two elements of legitimation of the sick role . . .
are conditional in highly important sense. It is relative legitimation so long as he (the patient) is in this unfortunate state which
both he and alter (significant others) hope he can get out of as
expeditiously as possible". The assumption is that the illness
and occupancy of the social position of the patient will be
temporary. This is certainly an appropriate assumption in
relation to acute illness conditions. But what of long-term,
chronic, or permanent illness conditions? Can occupancy of
the social position of patient be long-term, chronic, or permanent also?

The distinguishing characteristics of chronic or long-term
illness, and permanent disability or handicap depart in certain
crucial aspects from the Parsonian model of illness. However,

our response to this discrepancy is not to re-formulate, refine
or redefine Parsonian theory, or to fall into the trap of saying
that something is not "illness" because it does not conform with
Parsons' formulation. To do the first is outside the scope of this
book, it is in essence a sociologist's task for sociologists, while
to do the second is plainly rather absurd. A much more sensible
procedure is to see in what respects there is a discrepancy
between "widely held views" about "being a patient" and
typical instances where such ideas would seem not to fit the
case. Then, if such discrepancies are clearly defined, the next
task is to see whether or not actors in particular situations
perceive the discrepancy, and if they do not ask ourselves why
they do not, and if they do see in what way they resolve the
discrepancy in practice.

So, in the case of a person with a chronic or permanent
illness condition it is clear that, by definition, they cannot
conform to expectations based on assumed temporariness of
the condition. Similarly, since many chronically ill people are
ambulatory, incapacity for the performance of other roles is
often partial rather than total. Thus, the notion that the sick
role and being a patient will be the dominant role for the duration of the illness may well, in the case of the ambulatory
chronically ill person, be unwarranted.

A common response to such an incompatibility between,
on the one hand, having a chronic illness condition which
may be severe and, on the other hand, the wide-spread
notion that occupancy of the position of patient is temporary,
is a redefinition of the chronically symptomatic person's
"normal health". That is, the chronic condition gradually
becomes incorporated by the symptomatic person and
others into the definition of symptomatic person's "normal
health".

In the study of South Wales families, for example, Mrs B.[16]
had been waiting for four years to go into hospital for a heart
operation. This condition made her, among other things,
chronically and severely short of breath. Her range of activities
was very limited and she had to take drugs regularly to relieve

the worst of the symptoms. However, when asked, during one of a series of interviews, to describe the health of all the members of her family she described herself as "very healthy". Similarly Mrs I., who had a chronic, but controlled, kidney complaint which in the six months prior to answering the same question had necessitated two weeks in hospital, eight outpatient sessions, two visits to her doctor and eight visits from her doctor to her home, classified herself as "healthy most of the time".

This tendency to incorporate chronic incapacity into a definition of "normal health" is consistent with Gordon's work[17] where his respondents were presented with a series of illness descriptions and asked to say whether or not they would categorize a person with the condition as an "ill person". The descriptions most often identified as being of ill people were characterized by a serious, uncertain, or worsening prognosis. The next most often defined as ill were those who were in the process of being cured or with a controllable illness condition. Persons permanently disabled by a past condition or having a chronic condition were least likely to be classified as ill.

The idea that we modify our ideas about what we take to be the "normal health" of ourselves and other people and, thus, our ideas about when it is and when it is not appropriate to be "a patient" should not come as a great surprise. For we quite readily apply relative notions of good health with respect to people of different ages. The importance of the interplay between physical conditions and the social context in which those conditions are found is quite clear when we realize that it would be felt to be quite absurd to respond to the wheezing cough in a new born child in the same way as in a man of sixty. However, the fact that there are certain similarities between being ill and being old often leads to unwelcome consequences in the case of old chronically ill people. There is evidence[18] that older people with chronic illness conditions tend to tolerate various types of functional impairment unnecessarily, in that such impairments could be ameliorated with medical care, because of the erroneous association of the symptoms with aging rather than with illness.

Another major problem associated with chronic and permanent illnesses is that there are more opportunities for disagreement over the interpretation of conditions and concomitant action as being that of a patient or an ill person. In a situation where there is a greater deal of room for manoeuvre over definitions there will be more likely to be disagreements over the appropriate action by the symptomatic person and the appropriate response to him. It is often in the area of chronic and permanent illness that such notions as malingering, over-cautiousness, stoicism, foolhardiness, and irresponsibility, are employed. Malingering and over-cautiousness are common-sense notions used by some "other" to describe a symptomatic person who is deemed to be claiming unnecessarily the rights associated with the sick role. Stoicism, foolhardiness, and irresponsibility are common-sense notions used to describe a symptomatic person who is carrying-on when the condition is believed by "others" to be such that the symptomatic person's adoption of the sick role is warranted or commanded.[19]

Clearly, in any illness situation people will differ to a greater or lesser extent in their ideas about appropriate action by or towards the symptomatic person. In the case of chronic or permanent illness conditions when, as has been suggested earlier, the conception of the symptomatic person's "normal health" may be redefined, the opportunity is likely to be greater for disagreement and differences over what is to count as appropriate action.

Seeking help

The fourth major commonly accepted element of the sick role is that which obliges the sick person to seek technically competent help. This will usually, but not necessarily, be from a qualified doctor with whom the patient is also expected to co-operate to the best of his ability. While the condition lasts and the patient is doing all he can by way of co-operating with medical experts there is the obligation upon those about the patient to make his life as easy as possible and to facilitate the consultation, treatment, recovery and recuperation processes. Here again, therefore, is emphasized the impossibility of seeing the patient's position and action in isolation from the complementary, contradictory, competing, co-operating action of all those professional and lay others who are involved.

It is not possible in such a short piece to do anything more than just introduce certain perspectives and strong themes of interest and research concern. It is certainly beyond the scope of such a volume to do anything other than guide to the detailed discussion of variations in sick role conception related to social stratification,[20] cultural differentiation,[21] and certain individual differences.[22] Similarly, although this chapter is entitled "The Patient: a Social Position" and has for the most part concentrated upon the sick role it is entirely unsatisfactory to consider social actions solely in terms of individual's roles and their apparent responses to the normative requirements of particular social systems. As an antidote to this over-socialized conception of man as some kind of package pushed hither and thither at the demands of "society" it has been stressed how essential it is to recognize and take account of man's singularity in relation to any particular type of social situation. What is meant by the singularity of man is that he stands against society as he sees it as well as being incorporated within it. While the social position of any individual is inconceivable without any consideration of the particular social whole of which it is part, so the social whole is inconceivable without individuals in social positions. Further, since social wholes are the mental constructs of individual men and since individual men occupy social positions in varying numbers of social wholes it is clear that the individual is as determining *vis-à-vis* any particular social whole as determined.

It follows, therefore, that when we turn from "a patient" as a social position to a consideration, in Chapter IV, of "Patient and Doctor" we must not expect to find that their relationship is pre-ordained but will expect to find that it is open, to a greater or lesser extent, to negotiation, reinterpretation, mis-interpretation and disagreement. For that is what *social* life is all about.

Summary

The aim of this short chapter has been to re-focus attention upon the distinction between the possession of symptoms or illness conditions and the social concomitants of such posses-sion. Just as becoming a patient was seen as a process of bargain and manoeuvre so *being* a patient and performing the sick-role is a matter of mutual orientation between the symp-tomatic person and significant others.

Parsons'[23] delineation of major features of the sick role were presented. His formulation suggests that the person legitimately occupying the social position of sick person or patient is (1) exempt from certain normal social responsibilities; (2) cannot be expected to take care of himself or to get rid of his illness by "willpower"; (3) should want to get well; and (4) should seek medical advice and co-operate with medical experts. Clearly, in specific illness situations the ideas about appropriate be-haviour of those involved will accord to a greater or lesser extent with Parsons' formulation. However, since our concern is with everyday action, Parsons' formulation is not set up as a standard for action but merely as an example of the sort of thing which is implied in setting out the rights and duties associated with the occupancy of some social position such as patient.

In order to describe, offer explanations and indicate impli-cations of, social action in any particular illness situation it would be necessary to gain an understanding of the *actual* expectations about appropriate behaviour which informed the various people involved.

Suggestions for further reading:
Gordon, G. *Role Theory and Illness.* College & University Press, New Haven, Connecticut, 1966.

Kasl, S. V. and Cobb, S. Health Behaviour, Illness Behaviour and Sick Role Behaviour. *Arch. Environmental Health.*, 12, 246, 1966.

Parsons, T. *The Social System.* Free Press, Chicago, 1951. (Chapter X).

Sigerist, H. E. The Special Position of the Sick. *In* Roemer, M. I. *Sigerist on the Sociology of Medicine.* M.D. Publications, New York, 1960.

Twaddle, A. C. Health Decisions and Sick Role Variations: an exploration. *J. Health and Social Behaviour*, *10*, *105*, 1969.

CHAPTER IV

Patient and Doctor: a Social Relationship

"'Illness is something that happens between the doctor and the patient' (Valabrega). *He means by this that illness is not an autonomous entity, but a result of the confrontation of two individuals, the first contributing the mystery of his illness and the second proposing an explanation and fitting the subjective realm into the objectivity of a theoretical system. . . . However, the construction transcends the dialogue, since behind the patient is the whole weight of collective representations which he and his friends and relatives have of . . . illness, and behind the doctor are the systems he has learned in books and during his training. The therapeutic dialogue is therefore an exchange between two elements of society rather than two individuals."*

Bastide[1]

Chapter III concentrated upon certain features of the patient's position and the sick role. The discussion now widens to cover the relations between patients and others. The main thread which runs through this chapter is a consideration of the patient-doctor relationship. This particular relationship, however, cannot be considered without bearing in mind the context within which that relationship is set. It is not being suggested, of course, that the patient-doctor relationship is our only area of interest but rather that a consideration of it informs a great deal of the sociology of medicine and directs us to the heart of much of the everyday practice of medicine.

The notion of social relations was discussed in Chapter I and was seen to refer to the situation in which two or more people are engaged in conduct wherein, as Weber put it[2]:

> . . . in its meaningful content, the action of each takes account of that of the other and is oriented in these terms.

The social relation, thus, consists of the probability that individuals will behave in some meaningfully determined way. In other words, we come back to the question of expectations which people, occupying particular social positions, have concerning the actions of those in other related social positions. However, it must not be assumed that in every case, or even in most cases, there will be complete and harmonious reciprocity between one actor and another. Weber stressed this when he said, "a social relationship in which the attitudes are completely and fully oriented towards each other is really a marginal case".[3] The usefulness of the notion of social relations is that it directs our attention to important nuggets of social life. It helps us to see that "society" is not somehow a total phenomenon set over and against "the individual", and reminds us also that the individual is in dynamic interaction with other social beings and not simply either responding to overwhelming pressure or moulding some inert environmental mass.

The patient-doctor relationship

Like all patients, men of Ward F-Second were expected to entrust themselves to the physicians responsible for their care; to undergo the procedures that these physicians felt were necessary for the diagnosis and treatment of their conditions; to take the medications which had been prescribed for them; and, in general, to 'follow the doctor's orders'. As patients in a teaching hospital, they were expected to permit medical students and physicians other than their own to interview and examine them and sometimes to participate in their care. As patients on a research ward, they were under a certain amount of psychological and moral pressure to allow their physicians to try new procedures and drugs on them. Agreeing to do so meant accepting the hazards, the discomforts, and the rigorous controls conducting experiments on human subjects entails. *Fox*[4].

"Why, I met him in the drug store, and told him I had this pain in my left arm. He took me in the back room, and took my blood pressure and listened to my heart and all that . . . . Sure it was the same as an office call. . . . That goes on all the time. What's the sense of goin' around to spend time when you can catch him someplace". Respondent in *Koos*[5].

The discussion of the patient-doctor relationship will include first, an introductory discussion about what is commonly taken to be the nature of patient-doctor relations, and second, an indication of certain key features of doctor-patient relations and how these have been analysed. From clinical experience and from what has already been said in earlier chapters it is no surprise that doctors and patients may come together holding somewhat different conceptions of illness. The professional's views, moulded by clinical experience and training, may differ in emphasis, detail, or ordering of priorities, from the patient's views, influenced by the need to cope with a particular problem and by his cultural and social understanding of the nature of the problem and the range of possible responses to it. Thus, it is in the doctor-patient relationship that the lay and professional perspectives and priorities most intimately meet, accommodate each other, and clash. Having noted in Chapters II and III the variability of patient behaviour we must not forget that such variability does not take place against a background of professional certainty and conformity. Doctors too vary widely in their responses to illness situations, in their views of medicine and its relevance to a variety of problems and conditions, and in their training, experience, and philosophical perspectives. These points will be discussed more fully in Chapter V.

However, in spite of such variations in both lay and professional perspectives on illness, its definitions, and its management, when patients and doctors come together in a healing situation their actions are in a sense more ordered and predictable than in a situation when help may be offered or provided by friends or neighbours. The doctor, being a member of a particular professional group and practising within the context of a particular organizational setting whether it is a general practice, an industrial medical unit, a hospital or whatever, will have professional and organizational constraints upon the range of perspectives which are appropriate and options which are feasible. In other words, his actions are defined and confined by the law, professional ethics, time, space, inter-professional relations and the organization of medical practice. In addition, there are implications for the professional, in some systems of medical care, of being totally dependent upon the patient for economic livelihood.[6]

Apart from emergencies and acute stages of severe illness, any contact between a patient and his doctor is usually a result of a conscious choice on the part of the patient. It represents a decision on behalf of the patient in accordance with, or in spite of, the beliefs of his intimates that this course of action is preferable to other possible alternatives. It is certainly the case that such patient-initiated contact with the doctor may represent a desire as much for emotional support as for physical diagnosis or medication,[7] but for whatever the reason it is clear that the role of the doctor is widely regarded as encompassing two distinct facets. As Mechanic puts it[8]:

> Not only is the physician widely regarded as a man of knowledge and science capable of ferreting out the meaning of puzzling symptoms, but also he frequently is pictured as a kindly, thoughtful, warm person, deeply interested in and committed to the welfare of the individual.

The success of any particular patient-doctor interaction is likely to be evaluated by the patient in terms of the second facet of the doctor's role; namely, that the professional should be thoughtful, warm, interested and committed to the patient's welfare. The patient has few cues to assess the professional's technical medical scientific skill. He may admire the neatness of the sewing on an abdominal incision but is unlikely to be capable of assessing whether the incision was necessary, or if necessary whether it was made in the correct place, or if in the correct place whether what was done through it was carried out competently. In this situation, the patient's assessment of the professional's performance, upon which may rest in some degree the satisfactory outcome of the current episode or the liklihood of subsequent contact, will be based upon his view of such things as the doctor's interest in him, the amount of information given to him, the willingness of the doctor to show concern, to take an interest, and be "committed to the welfare" of the patient.

In particular cases, since each patient has his own definition of "commitment", the specific information which is given or not given, and the specific manifestations of concern which are shown or not shown, will depend upon how satisfactorily the patient indicates and the professional recognizes the cues of the situation. At whatever level, however, the compatibility of the expectations and performance of both the patient and the doctor has implications for the success of the relationship and, further, the outcome of the particular illness episode which brought them together.

Features of the patient-doctor relationship

In Chapter III the question was raised of how far and in what ways the patient was responsible for his condition and able to help himself. Earlier in this chapter it was pointed out that the patient and the doctor may bring to their interaction quite different perspectives as to the definition, development and likely outcome of the particular illness condition under discussion. But however different their perspectives on the condition, and however different their ideas about the patient's part in its genesis or its management, the patient and the doctor are likely to share certain ideas about the nature of their relationship with each other. At the very least they will tend to agree that the role of the doctor centres upon his responsibility for the welfare of the patient in the sense of facilitating his recovery from illness to the best of his ability. In meeting this requirement he is expected, and will accept, a responsibility to acquire and use competence in "medical science" and the relevant techniques based upon and associated with it. In short, the doctor-patient relationship is that of expert and layman. As such, the layman is dependent, by definition, upon the satisfactory exercise of specialist knowledge by the expert. The question of the acquiring of specialist knowledge and the issue of who, in what way exercises control over its application is discussed in Chapter V. However, as Friedson puts it, "when all is said and done . . . it is the physician's expertise which is his ultimate resource in his interaction with others".[9]

Whether or not we would want, in respect of medical expertise, to go along with Friedson's contention that:

> . . . neither expertise nor the expert who practises it has been examined carefully enough to allow intelligent and self-conscious formulation of the proper role of the expert in a free society. Indeed . . . expertise is more and more in danger of being used as a mask of privilege and power rather than, as it claims, as a mode of advancing public interest[10].

is a separate question which is merely raised here.

Since the position of patient *vis-à-vis* doctor is that of layman *vis-à-vis* expert it is also the case that the patient will be to a greater or lesser extent passive in the interaction. This is not to say, however, that all that doctors do is "the same" and requires the same type of interaction. Szasz and Hollander[11] have constructed a typology of doctor-patient relationships. Following it, we note that under certain circumstances – as in surgery and electro-convulsive therapy – the patient must be thoroughly immobilized and passive, wholly submissive to the activity of the doctor. The work itself requires minimal interaction: attendants, straps, anaesthesia, and other forms of restraint are employed to enforce the requirements of submissiveness. This model for interaction Szasz and Hollander call *activity-passivity*. In it the patient is a passive object.

The second treatment situation, and the one which conforms most nearly to the stereotype situation which most writers describe as *the* doctor-patient relationship is one in which the patient's consent to accept advice and follow it is necessary. Here, the patient:

> . . . is conscious and has feelings and aspirations of his own. Since he suffers . . . he seeks help and is ready and willing to

'co-operate'. When he turns to the physician, he places (him)
. . . in a position of power . . . the more powerful . . . will speak
of guidance or leadership and will expect the co-operation of the
other[12].

The interaction is expected to follow the model of *guidance-co-operation*, the physician initiating more of the interaction than the patient. The patient is expected to do what he is told by the expert, he assumes a less passive role than if he were anaesthetized but a passive role nonetheless, submissive to medical requirements as defined by the professional.

Third, there is the model of *mutual participation* found where patients are able or are required to take care of themselves – as in the case of some chronic illness conditions like diabetes. This type of interaction is found also where "the physician does not profess to know exactly what is best for the patient. The search for this becomes the essence of the therapeutic inter-action". Obviously some forms of psychotherapy can be included here.

Friedson takes Szasz and Hollander severely to task over their threefold typology of doctor-patient interaction.[13] He deems their scheme defective logically and empirically since the models represent only a continuum of the degree to which the *patient* assumes an active role in interaction, without being extended to the logical point where the doctor assumes a *passive* role. Logic dictates two further models of interaction – one in which the patient *guides* and the doctor *co-operates*, and one in which the patient is *active* and the doctor *passive*. While it is difficult to imagine an empirical instance of the latter logical possibility, it is possible to find contemporary and historical instances of the former. In a fee-for-service situation, particularly where the practice is economically unstable, it may certainly be the case that the patient guides and the doctor co-operates, while Duff and Hollingshead in Sickness and Society[14] present a detailed description of the way in which practitioners, due to their fear of losing status and income, were particularly responsive to their patients' demands for hospitalization and for acceptable diagnoses and types of treatment. But the point of discussing Szasz and Hollander's typology is not merely in order to describe features of ideal-type doctor-patient relationships but to draw attention to the necessity for discussions about the nature of such relations to be divorced from the question of "what the medical profession feel ought to be, or they would like to be, the case". On this point Friedson comments tartly that:

> This lack of concern for being logically consistent and systematic is characteristic of virtually all writing about the doctor-patient relationship by medical men . . . so long as medical writers persist in crippling their logic by normative considerations, they cannot expect serious intellectual consideration.[15]

What Friedson is saying is that just because some logical possibilities and empirical realities may be uncomfortable to admit to, or unlikely, or considered to be unprofessional, non-therapeutic or undignified is no excuse for excluding them from a typology or theory of some aspect of medical life or practice. Anyone with experience either as clinician or patient is aware that the viewpoints of the layman and the professional are never wholly synonomous. As such, there is always a measure of latent conflict in any patient-doctor relationship. Hence, it is often fruitful for the sociologist in his analysis of illness situations, and may also be fruitful for the clinician in his task of solving medical problems, to conceive of inter-action in treatment as a kind of negotiation. Balint suggests this when he describes the patient as using his symptoms to establish a relationship with the doctor.[16] But the notion of negotiation applies equally usefully to specific aspects of the patient-doctor relationship. As Roth's study clearly indicates,[17] just as the doctor may be struggling to find ways of withholding some kinds of information, so may the patient be struggling to find ways of gaining access to or inferring such information. The particular question of the communication of information in medical settings is discussed in Chapter VI.

Privileged access

Another core feature of the patient-doctor relationship is that of privileged access. It is one of the implications of a primary definition of the doctor's responsibility to "do everything possible" to aid the recovery of his patient. However, the doctor, unlike many other experts, often deals with human beings in a manner which outside the context of the patient-doctor relationship would be criminal, immoral, scandalous, or ridiculous.

As part of the doctor's task it is frequently necessary that the patient's body be exposed and touched, that access should be had to it, that it should be mutilated in some way or that its biochemical functioning should be interfered with. While such activities may become, through medical training and clinical experience, part of the professional's taken-for-granted perspective, it is clearly a source of possible conflict, tension, and upset for patients who must readjust their usual conception of appropriate behaviour in relation to their body.

To see a person naked when this is not usual and to touch and manipulate their body is a "privilege" which must be justified. In terms of the patient-doctor relationship this is usually done in terms of the need for the doctor to have access to the body in order to perform his function as someone "doing everything possible" for the patient's well being, whether this is in terms of prevention, diagnosis, or treatment. Such a justification is essential when some of the doctor's contacts, such as vaginal or rectal examinations, may not be permitted to any other person even a sexual partner. However, the justification of privileged access in order to diagnose or treat is, in the teaching hospital situation, extended to "privileged access in order to teach others" to be able to carry out their essential medical tasks at some time in the future.

The patient's usual notions of the "inviolability" of his body may have to be temporarily shelved when procedures, routine for the professional, such as the insertion of a hypodermic needle are contemplated. In other cases the doctor's access to the body is clearly seen to be not a right, by virtue of his position *vis-à-vis* the patient in some medical setting, but a privilege granted by formal consent of the patient, and the securing of consent to surgical procedures and certain types of diagnostic procedures – such as the use of a gastroscope or a bronchoscope – cannot be taken for granted. Parsons sums up this point by saying that:

> The essential point in all this is that these are not simple matters of weighing a rationally understood 'need' against an equally rationally assessed 'cost' in terms of discomfort or inconvenience, but very complex non- and irrational reactions are involved with the typical as well as the 'abnormal' patient. The fact that these elements are organized and controlled does not make them unproblematical.[18]

Again, the doctor in the course of a commonly-accepted performance of his task may need access to confidential information about his patient's life. The likelihood of his doing a competent medical job may depend upon gaining privileged access to intimacies which would otherwise be divulged to no-one. Taken together these various facets of exposure, touching, manipulation, mutilation, and learning intimacies, all go to make "privileged access" a core feature of the patient-doctor relationship. At whatever level physical, biochemical, psychological, or emotional the doctor, in order to perform his professional role, is inevitably going to be involved in significant "private" affairs of his patients. The kind of involvement will vary from case to case and situation to situation, but whatever its precise nature is a source of potential conflict for the patient and the doctor and a matter to be negotiated over.

The problem of uncertainty

> All physicians are confronted with problems of uncertainty. Some of these result from their own incomplete or imperfect mastery of available medical knowledge; others derive from limitations in current medical knowledge; and still others

grow out of difficulties in distinguishing between personal ignorance or ineptitude and the limitations of medical science[19] *Fox*.

"I really cannot tell if the nurses here are good or not. I've never been able to find out what they're supposed to be doing for me. . . . Sometimes I get my medicine every two hours on the dot. At other times it comes every two and a half hours. Is this somebody's mistake or is it the way the doctor wanted it? Hell, I don't know". Respondent in *Skipper*.[20]

The problem of uncertainty is something to be recognized in relation to all illness situations. We can distinguish at the outset for purposes of discussion, between certain *causes* of uncertainty, on the one hand, and the *handling* and *effects* of that uncertainty, on the other. Earlier chapters have highlighted the patient's uncertainty in relation to what signs count as symptoms of what illness conditions, when, in whom, and what should be done in response to them. However, the professional is also faced with acute problems of uncertainty.

For the doctor, the two main areas of uncertainty surround diagnosis and therapy. In any particular case certainty in one area has no one-to-one relationship with certainty in the other. A competent diagnosis may expose, with certainty, a particular illness condition but in relation to the condition there may be uncertainty about whether there should or should not be therapeutic intervention. Or if it is clear that there should be intervention it may be far from certain what, among a number of possible alternatives, the particular response should be. The development of medical science is not a progression of the removal of uncertainty. On the contrary cherished certainties are often undermined. For example, in the 1870s many people, both in the medical profession and outside it, had a strong faith in the efficacy of various drugs in the treatment of pneumonia. Sir William Ostler, one of the most eminent physicians of the day, undertook, against strong opposition, to show that such certainty was not well founded. He claimed that there was not a single case of the use of drugs in this condition which was not either useless or positively harmful. Sulfa drugs and penicillin had not been discovered at that time and the effect of Ostler's campaign was to reduce an area of contemporary certainty and yet to represent scientific advance.[21]

The handling of recognized uncertainty is a particularly important feature of doctor-patient interaction. The question of how far a member of the medical profession goes to confirm a suspected diagnosis is a constant fact of medical life. The patient and his family, for example, may know only that he has abdominal discomfort, has been losing weight and lacks energy. The diagnostic procedure reveals an advanced inoperable cancer of the stomach with a hopeless prognosis. More is "known" than before, the area of uncertainty is reduced, but hope may be removed. In such cases the question of whether or not the doctor reduces the patient's uncertainty by revealing the diagnosis is immediately raised. The problem of how to handle uncertainty is clearly acute. For the patient's part there may well be reluctance to consult about some disorder or discomfort for fear of the certainty of diagnosis which may result. Scheff[22] has noted that medical decision-making in circumstances of uncertainty is not vastly different in its basic logic from legal or statistical decision-making tasks. When a doctor searches for an illness to account for reported discomfort but has no positive findings he must choose between either further assessment and evaluation or calling off the diagnostic process. The risks associated with further exploration may be too high in terms of time, or facilities, the risk to the patient's health by the diagnostic procedures themselves, and the distress which further exploration may cause the patient in emotional, familial and perhaps economic terms. On the other hand, failure to continue may result in a failure to detect a potentially serious condition which requires early evaluation and treatment. Since many mild and self-limiting conditions present themselves in a fashion similar to the early stages of some serious ones, the doctor must develop strategies to handle such uncertain situations.

Since a primary expectation of the doctor is that he should do everything he can for his patients it can easily be the case in a situation of uncertainty, particularly where his uncertainty is shared by the patient and his family, that the doctor may be under great pressure to do *something*. He is himself trained and expected to act. There can on all sides be, in Pareto's terms, "a need to manifest sentiments by external acts". This situation is exemplified when a decision to operate is in the balance. As Parsons puts it:

> A surgeon must weigh the risk of operation against the risks of delay or of deciding not to operate at all. In general there tends to be a bias in favour of operating. After all, the surgeon is trained to operate, he feels active, useful and effective when operating. For the patient and his family, in their state of anxiety and tension also, inactivity, just waiting to see how things develop, is particularly hard to bear. A decision to operate will, in such a situation, almost certainly 'clear the air' and make everybody feel better.[23]

Just as, in the situation which Parsons outlines, the decision to operate may "clear the air" so in the same way a doctor's assurance that something is wrong may "clear the air" for the patient. In a study of decision-making in relation to illness in a small number of families, all wife-mothers were asked to keep a health diary.[24] Each day symptoms or upsets were noted for each member of the family together with a report of what action if any was taken. An extract from the "S family" health diary gives evidence of a build up of tension and concern until the family doctor made a pronouncement which "cleared the air".

Mrs S. was a very nervous, pregnant woman with one young child two years old. She had no formal secondary education because of long periods in hospital. At the time of this extract in the health diary Mrs S. was about seven months pregnant. This event, like many other events in her life, was something to be worried about and which she had difficulty in satisfactorily coping with. The family had moved to a new house on a private housing estate some months previously but Mrs S. had left the house only to go to the doctor. Mr S., a motor mechanic, did all the shopping and was a very harassed and, at times, exasperated man. The following extract from Mrs S's. health diary deals with her own symptoms and comments about them. After six days when no symptoms were reported Mrs S. entered the fact that her "nails are splitting badly". This was the beginning of a whole series of symptoms, worries and comments which were reported until day 12 when the doctor at the ante-natal clinic makes the vital comment which finishes the episode. In fact, all the doctor says is that Mrs S. is overweight and must "stop eating too much". However, the effect is sufficient to enable Mrs S. to go for seven days without mentioning any further symptoms for herself in the diary.

Extract from the S family health diary (build-up to doctor's comments)

Day	Symptom	Action taken	Comment
1	My nails are splitting badly		
2	Nothing		
3	My legs are swelling badly		Wish I had time to rest my legs more
4	My legs still swelling and nails splitting. I have had a lot of constipation lately	Taken laxative for constipation	
5	I still have Wednesday's symptoms		
6	I still have the same symptoms		
7	My body is feeling very weak and my nerves are still bad		
8	Just the same as Sat.		

Day	Symptom	Action taken	Comment
9	I have constipation	Taken laxatives	
10	I had very bad back and stomach pains before the laxatives work		
11	I had very bad wind in my back, eating far too much last week or so. But just can't stop myself	Had J (husband) to rub my back until wind came up.	
12	Now I have haemorrhoids	I went to ante-natal clinic. Told doctor my symptoms	Doctor told me I am overweight and must stop eating too much
13	Nothing		
14	Nothing		
15	Nothing		
16	Nothing		
17	Nothing		
18	Nothing		
19	Nothing		

When asked about this episode after the diary-month Mrs S. was quite explicit about how relieved she was to tell the doctor about her various symptoms. She also said that she was glad she knew what the cause was (overweight) after the visit, even though she had herself entered in the diary the fact that she was "eating far too much". When pressed on this she said how difficult it was to know what was important and what wasn't "when you get to being ill". After the doctor's visit, when she knew what the "real" problem was, the other symptoms—wind, constipation, backache and leg swelling—were not considered to be noteworthy.

The therapeutic procedures which a doctor may choose in any particular case may well be informed by a consideration of the familial and work situation of a patient. Thus, the question of uncertainty is often solved by making reference to the whole context of the patient's current or possible future relationships. The burdens which the doctor may ask the families of patients to bear are often very severe. The general practitioner is in the most advantageous position to establish the kind of relationship with the family as a whole which will enable him to make decisions about any particular ill member in respect of such things as the availability of help and sources of information, the most appropriate person with whom to discuss diagnosis and prognosis, and the likelihood of sympathetic understanding for the patient and co-operation with any particular form of treatment. It is in the light of such considerations that some of the uncertainties for the professional in particular illness situations can be resolved.

Clearly, the question of uncertainty is a constantly recurring feature of doctor-patient interaction. The causes of uncertainty, strategies for handling uncertainty, and the effects of uncertainty and its handling upon the mental and physical well-being of the patient are problems which are at the core of the practice of medicine. The next section deals with two intimately related questions.

"Non-diseases" and "non-medical problems"

Scheff[25] identifies a "bias towards illness" in situations of uncertainty and terms this tendency a medical decision-rule which holds that the professional, since he believes that the work he does is for the good of the client, typically assumes that it is better to impute disease than to deny it, or risk overlooking or missing it. Garland's study[26] of X-ray readings for tuberculosis, which show that of 14,867 films 1,216 were interpreted false positive while only twenty-four were interpreted false negative clearly revealed this tendency toward imputing illness rather than health. The tendency is supported by many other studies of diagnostic performance not only in the United States, whose medical professionals might be considered more likely to inflate the category of illness for financial reasons, but in Great Britain as well.[27]

As a corollary of such a medical decision-rule Meador draws our attention [28] to the notion and implications of a "non-disease". This he defines as a diagnostic label which is established after a person has been incorrectly diagnosed as ill of a particular disease, or suspected of having a disease and then after closer inspection is ruled not to have it. All false positives are non-diseases among which are a number of syndromes such as the mimicking syndrome, the normal-variation syndrome, and the laboratory-error syndrome. Meador's work is only semi-serious but, as is often the case, such presentations contain a kernel of profound truth which is foolish to ignore. Superficially, it would seem that having a "non-disease" is hardly more serious and involves nothing more than a certain amount of temporary worry and time wasted on one or more unnecessary visits to a surgery or clinic, while the medical decision-rule argues that it is more serious to miss a diagnosis by carelessness, ignorance or accident than to temporarily diagnose one.

However, the assumption is that the diagnosis *is* temporary. What is overlooked is that since illness, as well as being a bio-physiological disturbance, has a *social* meaning also, the designation of illness is not solely supplied or controlled by the medical profession. Some "illnesses" may not be undone or become non-diseases in the world of the patient just because they have become so in the world of the professional. A case of "alcoholism" or "mental illness" or any suspected illness which could legitimately be inferred from the fact of a referral to an alcoholism out-patient clinic or a psychiatric hospital may come into the category of stigmatized conditions[29] which are rather more difficult to get rid of than being "cleared of" suspected measles or pneumonia.

Such implications of "non-diseases" highlight again the importance of the consideration of a whole range of social meanings which an illness episode has for all the participants to it. The disjunction between the patient's viewpoint and that of the professional is a question which needs to be understood in relation to a complaint often made by the professional that "patients insist on bringing non-medical problems". Such a complaint is often heard from those members of the profession who conceive of their task "as doctor" largely in terms of the exercise of technical scientific expertise. When confronted with a variety of emotional and psycho-social problems the tendency may be to define them out of the sphere of medical competence as "non-medical" problems, while another practitioner may accept them as in their very essence medical. Clearly, an explanation of why particular patients and doctors define particular problems as medical or not medical is vital to any understanding of social action in relation to any illness situation. But the explanation of particular situations will only be possible after gaining an understanding of how the participants themselves see the nature of the medical task, and what features of the doctor-patient interaction are given particular emphasis. In other words, the explanation will only be possible by placing the situation in its socio-cultural context.

Certain points can be made, however, about why it is that the question of what is a medical problem is increasingly being posed. One body of thought contends that it is a consequence of the increased bureaucratization of many aspects of life which have accompanied industrial change in the past decades. It is suggested that as opportunities for close personal contact diminish, as populations become increasingly geographically mobile, so problems which have previously been handled in familial, neighbourhood and religious contexts are increasingly being transferred to the formal helping professionals such as social workers and doctors.[30] As the structure of the patient-doctor relationship allows an opportunity for expressing intimacy and requesting help so it is natural that various emotional and psycho-social problems should be presented to the doctor which he may or may not see as part of his task to deal with.

Similarly, a core feature of the patient-doctor relationship is, as was discussed in an earlier section, the fact of the professional's privileged access to various types of intimacy in order to facilitate the conduct of the diagnostic or therapeutic task. Since it is impossible to entirely separate the technical scientific from the intimate aspects of the relationship, as far as the professional's usual definition of his own task is concerned, it is natural that the patient may over estimate the professional's interest and readiness to deal with the intimate psycho-social problems of living.

Other experts

> "I don't know what we'd do without the druggist. He's a sort of second doctor in our family . . . he helped a whole lot of people out of a hole many times." Respondent in *Koos*. [31]

> The chiropractor, the spiritual healer, the christian science practitioner, and many other helpers are frequently more attuned to the psychological needs of their client, and often the theories of disease they advocate are culturally and psychologically consistent with the views and hopes of their clients. *Mechanic*.[32]

The discussion up to now in this chapter has focused entirely upon the relationship between the patient and the traditional medical practitioner. But the range of alternative sources and types of help to the patient, for those diseases and discomforts usually taken to the professional medical practitioner, is wide. It has been argued[33] that, despite the attacks of the Medical Associations designed to eliminate them, competing systems of disease classification and health care have persisted and continued to be recognized, and used in part because the doctor has frequently failed to use effectively his role in the treating of the whole man.

The neighbour, the friend, the home compendium, and the chemist, all play their part "as experts", by virtue of experience or authority or expertise in respect of the patient and his illness. The source and nature of advice about diagnosis, the cause of an illness condition, and appropriate responses to it, must all be taken into account if action in any particular of the situation is to be understood. However, it is likely that the sources of expert aid and advice just mentioned would see themselves as operating largely in the context of, and in support of, a traditional scientific medicine.

But what of competing diagnostic and therapeutic systems such as those of the herbalist, the chiropractor or the faith healer? The absolute rightness of one system of medical theory of illness as opposed to another is not a very helpful question to ask. However, the *usefulness* of one theory in comparison with another is a more sensible question since particular uses can be stated and the value of various theories as predictors of particular outcomes can, within certain limits, be discussed. Thus, it might be argued that the value of medical biological theories over primitive religious theories is that they more effectively locate the nature of specific illness conditions and suggest more viable remedial measures.

The logic of the diagnostic models of folk and spiritual healers may be identical with those of modern scientific medicine. The patient may complain of some distress, the healer identifies a particular disfunction and his theory indicates certain remedial measures designed to correct the disfunction and relieve the distress. Whether the procedure is best under-pinned by the belief that the disfunction is a consequence of biochemical abnormality, spiritual failing on the part of the patient, or due to possession by evil spirits, is to be judged not *a priori*, but by attempting to make some assessment of the soundness of the predictions such a theory makes as to satisfactory outcome.

Clearly any explanation of social action in any particular illness situation must be firmly based upon and must not violate those common-sense assumptions about the nature of health and illness in terms of which such action is oriented.

Summary

This chapter has concentrated upon the relationships between the patient and the doctor, and sought to show how any understanding is impossible without a consideration of the context within which the relationship is set. Since the process of becoming a patient is, as was shown in Chapter II, a social process, and since the medical practitioner comes to occupy that position as a result of another long and complicated socialization process, the therapeutic encounter between them is, as Bastide puts it, "an exchange between two elements of society rather than two individuals".[34]

After an indication of what is commonly taken to be the nature of the patient-doctor relationship, certain features of the relationships were discussed. The notion of privileged access was cited as a core feature of the interaction and was seen to be derived from the commonly accepted responsibility of the medical practitioner to "do everything possible" to aid the recovery of his patient. Privileged access was taken to refer to certain procedures undertaken by the practitioner as part of his taken-for-granted activity which outside the context of the patient-doctor relationship would in all probability be deemed criminal, immoral, scandalous, or ridiculous.

Uncertainty was seen to be a feature of most illness situations. For purposes of discussion certain causes of uncertainty were distinguished from the handling and effects of that uncertainty. The chapter ended by focusing upon the definition and implications of "non-disease" and "non-medical problems", and indicated the part played by experts other than the traditional medical practitioner.

Suggestions for further reading:

Balint, M. *The Doctor, his Patient and the Illness*. Tavistock Publications, London, 1964.

Freidson, E. Client Control and Medical Practice. *Amer. J. Sociol.*, 65, 374, 1960.

Koos, E. *The Health of Regionville: what the people thought and did about it*. Columbia University Press, New York, 1954.

Mechanic, D. *Medical Sociology*. Free Press, New York, 1968.
Zola, I. K. Illness behaviour of the working class: implications and recommendations. *In* Shostak A. B. and Gomberg, W. (Eds.) *Blue Collar World*. Prentice-Hall Inc. Englewood Cliffs, New Jersey, 1964.

CHAPTER V

Medicine: a Particular Profession

> "*The town banker, a successful businessman, the resident manager of a local manufacturing plant, the doctor, the minister . . . (p)ossessing the security of a salary or income from their own businesses, having special educational qualifications, or wearing 'the halo of a profession' . . . were definitely set apart in their own minds and in the minds of others as important members of the community*".
>
> Koos[1]

Social action in any particular situation is informed and given meaning by those ideas about self and others in terms of which the participants structure the world about them. In illness situations one recurrent theme, or set of widely held ideas, concerns the notion of the doctor as "a professional". The word has been used in earlier chapters without elaboration, or footnotes, or definition. It is, clearly, a commonly used notion which is handled with little difficulty. But our ability to understand action in particular illness situations depends upon, among other things, our ability to determine what the notion of "professional" is commonly taken-for-granted to mean to the medical practitioners and the laymen involved. In what way is "being a member of a profession" different from being a member of a non-professional occupational group? What implications do such differences have for the practitioners and for laymen? This chapter raises some of the problems involved in the definition of "a profession" and indicates some of the particular features of "the professional" in relation to the practice of medicine.

While, as Friedson says,[2] "it is difficult to find much agreement on a definition of the word 'profession'", it is also the case that the members of a great many occupational groups apply it to themselves. This state of affairs, in which the word has been applied to a wide variety of occupational groups has

led Becker,[3] among others, to claim that it is hopeless to
expect the word to refer to more than a social symbol which
people attach to some occupations and not to others. From
such a position, however, it would be quite possible to study
the process of negotiation between some occupational group
and the rest of society over the former's claim to be a profession,
and then to construct a definition of "a profession" in terms
of the assumptions underpinning such negotiations. Another
strategy would be to discover which occupations are by
common consent "professions" and then, if possible, to abstract
certain common characteristics which appear to differentiate
them from other occupational groups.

But whatever our strategy, we should not be surprised to
encounter widely divergent views about what were the key
defining features of a profession. In short, we would not expect
to find that commonly held ideas of what counts as a profession
are so unanimous that journal articles with titles such as "Is
social work a profession?",[4] or "The Librarian: from occupation to profession?"[5] will cease to appear.

Occupations

However professions are defined, their members are only
part of a larger division of labour which includes a variety of
other occupations which are also concerned in one way or
another with the purposes and tasks with which the professional
is concerned. The precise way in which domains of work,
whether or not they are considered professional, are divided up
in the division of labour appears really quite arbitrary. For
example, in modern medicine it is quite arbitrary to separate
compounding, dispensing, prescribing and diagnosing. On the
other hand, is there any reason why diagnosing should not be
separated from cutting, thereby making a surgeon someone
who merely "cuts to order", as the pharmacist "dispenses to
order" or the nurse "injects to order?" Clearly, what particular
tasks go to make up a job, or an occupation, or a profession
are not God given, natural or inevitable.

We can distinguish between the sociology of professions on the one hand and the social aspects of medicine, law, or any particular occupational group on the other. The former provides a limited view of any single profession but attempts a broad, abstract, comparative view. The latter provides a concrete, detailed view of a single occupational group. The latter is, for the profession concerned, likely to be the most immediately relevant and useful approach, but the former has its uses. The sociology of professions provides a broad perspective which can serve as an intellectual counterbalance to any single profession's commitment to itself, to its own self-conception, to its special paradigms or points of view, to its occupational priorities and ambitions, its notions of its rightful place in society and its views of what should count as appropriate relations with others. The professional, for his part, by addressing himself to what the sociologists of professions postulate, can keep the abstractions honest and relevant by raising questions of logic and specialist detail.

The prestige of occupations

The role of medical practitioner is usually taken to belong to the general category of professions, a sub-class of the larger category of occupations. In sociology itself the family, the church the school and the community have long been central areas of interest. Nevertheless, the importance of occupations as a means of social classification and differentiation has always been recognized. Such questions as "how is the relative rank of each occupation determined and what implications does it have for particular categories of people?", "to what extent are occupations inherited?", "why do we find variations among occupational groups in political attitude, life expectancy, interests, insanity, family size?", "to what extent is an occupational group able to regulate its own activities?", are regularly posed.

Several problems face anyone who addresses himself to any

of these or similar questions. First, occupations differ in definiteness. The learned professions, the organized crafts and certain trades like policemen, bus-conductor, tailor and waitress are readily defined and relatively easily recognized. Others are identified with less certainty. Such occupations as vitrifier or flow analyst are too unfamiliar to be defined at all by many people. Administrative consultant and company director are particularly unspecific and vary greatly in terms of specific job content from one organization to another. Several occupations cover a wide range of activities and as such are not easily assigned to any position relative to other occupations in terms of such things as technical expertise or prestige. Farmer, for instance, covers the Scottish crofter and the millionaire Texas rancher. A further problem is that it is necessary to be clear about the unit of analysis which is being considered in relation to any particular question. Should we consider typists as a separate occupational group, or include them among clerical workers, or regard them as forming part of the vast category of non-managerial workers?

All these questions and definitional difficulties must be faced by those who attempt to study occupational groupings, and by those who attempt to make comparisons between occupational groupings in terms of level of skill, prestige, particular rewards, political power or whatever. Many writers in the field of medical sociology, epidemiology and social medicine employ classifications of occupations to stand for some notion of social class. That is, they employ a scale, often the Registrar General's Classification of Occupations,[6] in order to divide up the community in some say, and, then relate this categorization to some medical, clinical or behavioural fact or observation.

The assumption underlying the use of such a classification is that in some way, often never considered, it reflects meaningful distinctions between categories of people in the general population. The phrase "middle-class" is often used to refer to anyone who lives in a household whose head has some non-manual occupation. Working-class, thus, applies to anyone who lives in a household whose head has a manual occupation. Differences in exposure to or response to particular diseases or illness conditions are then explained in terms of discovered differences in the occupational status of particular categories of respondents, or patients or subjects. Unfortunately, much epidemiological work, particularly in the field of mental illness where the value of its application has yet to be demonstrated, often goes no further than the reporting of associations between some reported symptom or response and "social class" as measured by some occupational status scale.

The detailed debate about how satisfactory it is to equate social class with occupational prestige is merely referred to here.[7] However, the question of whether or not it is helpful to use a scale at all which assumes that occupational prestige is uni-dimensional can be briefly discussed. By and large, four assumptions appear to underlie almost all occupational status scales.

1. Non-manual work is superior to manual work.
2. Self-employment is superior to employment by others.
3. Clean occupations are superior to dirty ones and
4. Personal service is degrading and it is better to be employed by an enterprise than to be employed in the same work by a person.

The question is immediately raised of how much these assumptions accord with the assumptions of those people whose behaviour in particular situations is meant to be made more understandable by the use of such scales? For if there is little agreement with the assumptions underlying the scale then any explanation based upon its use is little less than meaningless. A second question concerns the possibility of constructing a single occupational scale which simultaneously attempts to satisfy all these assumptions. While most, but not all, scales place consultant surgeons "high" and street sweepers "low" they are not at all consistent in their assignment of the relative prestige of intermediate occupations. As Caplow puts it[8]:

There are certain inescapable dilemmas . . . which haunt the
architects of occupational scales and which have been resolved
by a variety of makeshifts. For example:
1. Should professional persons or business executives be given
    the highest rating?
2. Should all white-collar workers be placed above all manual
    workers, or should the two categories overlap? If so, by
    how much?
3. Should an occupational scale qualify the description of
    each category by data of income, size of community, or
    property ownership?
4. Where should professional burglars, fortune tellers, . . .
    gamblers, prostitutes, . . . be classed? Should they be
    arranged in a hierarchy of skill? How about apprentice
    gamblers and part-time prostitutes?
5. At what point in the scale do public employees become
    public officials?
6. Should butlers, nursemaids, and other skilled servants be
    classified as unskilled because personal services are de-
    grading? If so, why should chiropodists enjoy higher status
    than hairdressers?
7. What distinctions must be drawn between artisan-
    employees and artisan-proprietors? Is there a real distinc-
    tion between foremen who are skilled in the work they
    supervise and those who are not?
8. Do rich farmers engage in the same occupation as poor
    farmers?
9. Should the owner of a junk yard be considered an executive?
    Is a strip-teaser a professional worker? If not, where should
    they be grouped?

Professions

Strip-teasers notwithstanding, there are certain features of
occupational structure and activity which are commonly
associated with "professional" occupations. Many people
have addressed themselves to the issue of which criteria are
essential for an occupation to be a profession. Cogan[9] provides
a wide ranging, scholarly, review of such presentations while
Goode, under the provocative title "Encroachment, Charlatanism and the Emerging Profession: psychology, medicine
and sociology", draws our attention to two "core character-

istics" of professions from which, he maintains, other frequently cited characteristics are derived.[10] The two core characteristics are "a prolonged specialized training in a body of abstract thought" and "a collectivity or service orientation". Of these two traits Goode says that an occupation "may rank high on one but low on another. Thus, nursing ranks high on the variable of service orientation but has been unable to demonstrate that its training is more than a low-level medical education".

Goode derives ten characteristics of professions from the two core characteristics already mentioned. These are:

1. The profession determines its own standards of education and training.
2. The student professional goes through a more far-reaching adult socialization experience than the learner in other occupations.
3. Professional practice is often legally recognized by some form of licensure.
4. Licensing and admission boards are manned by members of the profession.
5. Most legislation concerned with the profession is shaped by that profession.
6. The occupation gains in income, power and prestige ranking and can demand higher calibre students.
7. The practitioner is relatively free of lay evaluation and control.
8. The norms of practice enforced by the profession are more stringent than legal controls.
9. Members are more strongly identified and affiliated with the profession than are members of other occupations with theirs.
10. The profession is more likely to be a terminal occupation. Members do not care to leave it, and a higher proportion are certain that if they had to do it over again they would again choose that type of work.

These characteristics are closely interdependent. More importantly they are all expressed as relationships; they assert obligations and rights between client and professional, professional and colleague, and professional and some formal agency. It is not being maintained by Goode that these characteristics are *only* found in professions but rather that such are the features of those occupations which usually answer to the name of profession. Further, any occupation which is striving to gain what it takes to be professional status usually aims to make such features the characteristics of its structure and activity.[11]

Freidson,[12] in "Profession of Medicine", extracts from Goode's formulation what he sees to be the strategic distinction between the professions and other occupations, namely, "legitimate organized autonomy". Five of Goode's "derived characteristics" (1, 3, 4, 5, and 7) refer to autonomy. The following extended quotation summarizes Freidson's position and it is this position and Freidson's work in general which informs much of what follows in this chapter.

> . . . a profession is distinct from other occupations in that it has been given the right to control its own work. Some occupations, like circus jugglers and magicians, possess a *de facto* autonomy by virtue of the esoteric or isolated character of their work, but their autonomy is more accidental than not and is subject to change should public interest be aroused in it. Unlike other occupations, professions are *deliberately* granted autonomy, including the exclusive right to determine who can legitimately do its work and how the work should be done. Virtually all occupations struggle to obtain both rights, and some manage to seize them, but only the profession is *granted* the right to exercise them legitimately. And while no occupation can prevent employers, customers, clients, and other workers from evaluating its work, only the profession has the recognised right to declare such 'outside' evaluation illegitimate and intolerable.[13]

Clearly, an occupation does not just find itself in a position of professional autonomy, nor does it gain such a position merely by making claim to it. A study of the history of particular occupations is well beyond the scope of this text[14] but a profession could only attain such a position of autonomy by virtue of "the protection and patronage of some elite segment of society which has been persuaded that there is some special value in its work".[15] Once a profession is established in its protected position of autonomy it is likely to have a dynamic of its own, but if its work comes to have little relationship to the knowledge and values of the wider society in which it is set it may have difficulty surviving. The profession's privileged position is given by, not seized from, the society. The practice of medicine occupies such a privileged position.

Medicine as a particular profession

In Chapter I it was suggested that to say that medicine is concerned with health and illness is not very helpful. For while it is true, it neither tells us what medical science is nor what medical practitioners do. In short, such a definition or description is so wide ranging that it would include everything from individual practices of self-diagnosis on the one hand to the researches of the biochemist on the other. In this chapter, therefore, we are considering medicine in so far as that word refers to an occupation whose members are concerned to diagnose and treat the illness conditions of those who consult them for such help. Medicine is, in this sense, as Freidson puts it[16] "an organized consulting occupation which may serve as the discoverer, carrier, and practitioner of certain kinds of knowledge".

The profession of medicine is dominant in terms of both prestige and expert authority. The medical profession's knowledge about illness conditions and their handling is readily accepted as definitive. While there are other systems of medical explanation such as those of the chiropractor or faith healer there are no representatives of such systems who hold official policy making positions in relation to health affairs. Western medicine is, thus, an occupation of high prestige, and authoritative pre-eminence.

Medicine is also a body of knowledge. The medical profession is concerned primarily to apply rather than generate knowledge. It was stressed in the introduction how the knowledge of medicine grows by accretion from the work of theorists in many different disciplines, and that at heart the medical professional is a man of action. That is to say, medical work is geared primarily to the solution of the concrete problems of individuals. As opposed to the theoretical work of the scientist in a particular discipline the medical practitioner *applies* the results of many disciplines in any particular instance. While the practitioner applies general principles to deal with concrete problems the scientist investigates concrete problems in order to *construct* general principles. It is one of the characteristics of the medical practitioner at work that he is obliged to carry on in the face of insubstantial or incomplete knowledge and *act* in relation to any particular case. While the sociologist or the biochemist, for instance, may discuss the relative merits of their theories of alcoholism, the medical professional actually has to do something *vis-à-vis* the person who presents himself with some alcohol-related problem. The medical decision cannot wait upon the outcome of the scientific debate. This is a built-in characteristic of all applied sciences and is, clearly, intimately linked with the question of uncertainty which was discussed in Chapter IV.

Autonomy

Every clinician is given, or assumes, authority within bounds which depend upon his possession of a body of knowledge, competence in what he undertakes, and a discipline which implies rules with regard to what he does *not* do and what lies *without* his competence. However, the extent of bounds of competence has always been a matter of discussion and debate. Burton, in 1621, in "The Anatomy of Melancholy", apologized for his presumption in dealing with this subject, "I being a divine have meddled with physick" but justified himself by saying "it is a disease of the soul on which I am treat, and as much pertaining to a divine as to a physician".[17]

But, whatever the precise area of professional competence, it is clear that professional autonomy is not absolute. The State has ultimate sovereignty and the relative autonomy of particular sections of it, like medicine, is conditional upon the agreement of representatives of "society as a whole". The precise bounds of professional autonomy vary from country to country. Usually at the heart of the medical professional's autonomy is its control over technical judgment. In some countries, such as the United States,[18] the professional may also have a great deal of control over the organization of medical practice, while in others, such as Great Britain,[19] or the Soviet Union[20] control over terms of practice is embodied in a series of laws.

While the profession's autonomy is dependent upon the State for its creation and maintenance, the professional, granted autonomy in respect of medical technique if not its organization, can command resources and exercise control over non-medical-technical aspects of life. The professional frequently serves as a gate-keeper to resources such as hospital facilities or particular drugs as well as to social categories such as "sick employee deserving of sickness benefit" or "satisfactory insurance risk". Such power and authority is deemed appropriate insofar as it is contingent upon the performance of technically competent work. By and large it is only a fellow professional who will be in a position to say no to particular claims.

Chapter IV emphasised the degree of manoeuvre which was possible in the patient-doctor relationship. The discussion of the medical practitioner "as professional" emphasises areas over which the patient has less power vis-à-vis the doctor's autonomous position. The language of the marketplace is often used to describe aspects of the doctor-patient relationship. But while words such as cost, benefit, and bargain can helpfully aid a description of certain aspects of social action in these situations the analogy should not become too pervasive. Feldstein[21] characterizes the distinction between the commercial and the medical "market place" in the following way:

The physician, not the patient, combines the components of care into a treatment. In other markets the consumer, with varying degrees of knowledge, selects the goods and services he desires from the available alternatives. In medical care, however, the patient does not usually make his choice directly. . . . He selects a physician who then makes . . . choices for him.

Freidson succinctly amplifies this description by saying that:

It is as if the housewife could choose the store she wished to patronise but not which of the articles in the store she could buy. The choice is made for her by those who run the store on the basis of their conception of what she "really" needs which may be no articles at all, articles she does not want, or, if she is lucky, just what she wants.[22]

Recruitment and education

Autonomy of operation in relation to the recruitment of new members and their education are central activities for any profession. The entire educational process, from the initial choice of candidates for training to the conferment of honours at retirement, is under the close control of the professional group itself. Similarly, the violation of occupational monopoly is punishable as a crime, thus emphasising that the State not only permits but helps to maintain the profession's autonomous position. Such a position is, in essence, different from those occupations which, striving for the status of profession, construct elaborate training and registration facilities which are not backed by law.

Certification from an Institute of Personnel Management or Hairdressing may indicate to other members of the occupation and to laymen that its possessor has undergone some form of training, and this fact may crucially inform the action of the significant others. But there is a clear difference between occupationally controlled certification backed by law, as in the case of medicine, which is a necessary condition of employment in the occupation, and certification, as in the case of personnel management and hairdressing, which at the moment is not.

Several studies of medical education[23] have concentrated upon major sociological interests such as the socialization into a particular system of values considered intrinsic to the practice of medicine,[24] learning to handle crisis situations such as death routinely, specialty choice,[25] career expectations,[26] social background,[27] and the relationship of any with each.[28]

Medical students, as has been stressed before, are confronted by a wealth of detail and an armoury of perspectives based upon different disciplines considered relevant to their applied practice of medicine. In response to this wide-ranging and often competing set of ideas and data Becker, in "Boys in White"[29] argues that the students orient their experience as trainee practitioners in terms of two core values. These values, strongly emphasised by the staff, are *medical responsibility*: "for the patient's well being . . . the physician is most a physician when he exercises this responsibility"[30] and *clinical experience* "actual experience in dealing with patients and disease" which acknowledges that medical diagnosis and treatment rest upon the application of muti-discipline based knowledge which can only be learned by doing it. Just as the good cook "knows" the correct balance of ingredients and their manipulation without reference to a recipe, and indeed in a way which could not in its entirety be captured in a subsequent description, so the practice of medicine is over and above the application of accumulated knowledge as expressed in "the text". An over-emphasis on this particular feature of medical practice results, as Becker observed in relation to the medical school which he studied, in a situation in which "argument from experience was quite commonly used and considered unanswerable. . . ." In such a situation "the only counter-argument that can prevail is by someone who can claim greater experience in the area discussed".[31]

As a potential man of action in a situation characterized by uncertainty and lack of exact or definitive knowledge, the medical student will learn to be a pragmatist. He will learn to rely on "feelings" and "results" rather than theory. Sharaf and Levinson[32] noted in their study of psychiatrists in training that "the dangers of 'intellectualizing' and 'book learning' are stressed. The highest value is placed on emotional experience, and widening the range of the 'gut response' as a means of understanding what is going on in oneself and in the patient."

Control

It was pointed out earlier that the profession's autonomous position was not only protected by but granted by the State. But in addition to the control of the State over the definition of the extent of professional autonomy, the profession exercises control over its own members. Two intimately related questions lie at the heart of a consideration of control; the evaluation of merit and professional ethics. In relation to the evaluation of merit the questions to be asked are very simple. Who evaluates what, how? The determination of merit is entirely in the hands of fellow professionals, at least in principle. In practice, the judgment of clients and of the general public needs also to be taken into account. Among the formal symbols of merit, conferred by fellow professionals, are honorific titles and rewards, membership in institutes, the right to specialize, and office holding in the controlling professional societies. Less formal symbols, but equally important, are the allocation of positions in particular practices and organizations and in the dominant systems of consultation and referral.

What is evaluated is a kind of technical expertise, but also much more than that. It is assumed first, that any practitioner is perfectly qualified to perform any ordinary duties of the profession but second, "that professionals are, like poets or sculptors, perfectly non-interchangeable, the work of each being a free creation of his personality".[33] Merit, is therefore, closely bound up with ideas of the professional's unique ability gained through practical clinical experience as well as through formal learning. Deference is paid by one professional making reference to another for consultation. The prestigious members of a profession are the "consultants" who thank, often in the most flowery language, their colleagues for sending work to them. The act of referral is, thus, an act closely bound up with a system of merit and prestige. This will be discussed further in Chapter VII.

Control of occupational behaviour is something which the members of all occupations exercise for themselves to a greater or lesser extent. In the case of crafts, the rules may sometimes be set down in a manual, which often preserves the terminology of the guild system. For the factory trades, the rules and regulations are chiefly those imposed by management. In the professions, the major rules are set down in codes of ethics. The importance of the code of ethics lies in the fact that its acceptance has the effect of establishing a whole series of relationships between practitioners and clients, practitioners and practitioners, and between practitioners and the State.

The most ancient and well known statement of occupational ethics is, of course, the oath of Hippocrates which embodies all the essential elements of the code of practice. These are[34]

1. To advance the profession rather than the individual practitioner.
2. Never to use the specialist knowledge or privilege to injure but always to help the client.
3. To defer to specialist assistance whenever this is in the best interests of the client and
4. To maintain professional secrecy.

While each of these principles is still considered important by both the professional and non-professional, there has been in recent years an attempt to bring the Hippocratic code up to date. The result has been the production of an International Code of Medical Ethics adopted in London in 1949, and also four Declarations. The first of these, the Declaration of Geneva (1948) is a pledge, designed for the occasion of newly-qualified doctors' admission to the medical profession. The Declarations of Helsinki (1964), Sydney (1968) and Oslo (1970) lay down recommendations regarding clinical research, the diagnosis of death and therapeutic abortion.

The sociologist's interest in the question of medical ethics is focused upon the interpretation and invocation of particular principles in relation to particular medical practical situations. The question of who supports whom in relation to which ethical questions and what are the implications of their alliance is a question of particular interest and importance. For while a code or declaration is a public standard it is, like the constitution of the United States, a standard which must be interpreted in practice.

A group of practitioners suggested in the British Medical Journal[35] that members of the medical profession should support liberal abortion, among other things, to control over-population. Lord Brock retorted that such an attitude was a departure from the old patient-centred code. "We shall have to decide," he wrote[36] "if we want to change the Hippocratic code to include a social code." The relationship between medical and social codes is discussed later in the section dealing with medical as an institution of social control. But it is clear that the interpretation of particular ethical principles lies at the heart of what is taken to be appropriate medical practice. But while the law includes the provision of severe penalties in the case of malpractice, for instance in relation to the carrying out of abortions in unlicensed clinics, and professional medical associations have elaborate disciplinary procedures, these are clearly not the primary mechanisms for ensuring appropriate conduct on the part of the practitioner.

Caplow, writing of the fact that the professions and crafts are usually felt to have more "freedom" than factory workers or retail traders, identifies the importance of internalizing the norms of appropriate conduct.

> The longer the period of occupational formation, the more completely are the rules assimilated and internalized in habits, and at the same time the greater will be the participants self-identification with the occupational group. In the end, he may cease to feel the rules as something imposed from without, and will regard them as his own motives. The greater the individual's

identification with the agency which imposes the rules, the less will be his resistance to them. In the case of the professions, this identification is well-nigh complete, even where the professional association is actually manipulated by a closed clique.[37]

In a debate about the possibility and value of teaching and internationally agreeing medical ethics, Jackson lays great store by the force of practical example.

A code is . . . a useful text from which to teach medical ethics. Such instructions can be given in lectures . . . and, even better, demonstrated in action. The value of example is nowhere more apparent than in the realm of medical ethics. The actions of the teacher in his dealings with patients speak louder than words. His personal integrity and high principles, his transparent honesty in diagnosis and treatment, his genuine concern for the well-being of his every patient – will be recalled by the young practitioner facing his lonely problem years later.[38]

The question of the evaluation of merit and the interpretation of ethical principles lie at the heart of any consideration of control in relation to medical practice. An attempt to understand social action in any particular illness situation must take into account the relevance of such questions for the orientation, in relation to that particular situation, taken by both the professional and the layman. It is one of the key dimensions in the whole constellation of dimensions which go to make up the common-sense notions of an appropriate relationship between people who occupy particular social positions.

Professionals and para-professionals

The relationships between one professional group and another are often less close than between other occupations of similar status. This is due, in part, to the fairly tight enclosure of particular professional worlds. The development of common intra-professional attitudes is reinforced in several ways; by the distinction which is drawn between co-professionals and laymen in every working situation, by the lengthy educational period, by the fixed organizational basis of the majority of the professional's career, and by the informal associations outside working times which are often tacitly required. In hierarchically organized career structures predominantly influenced by the elders, such as in medicine, young and even middle-aged professionals enter into *quasi-filial* relationships with older men who guide and sponsor them, and who set standards of personal as well as professional conduct.

Such mechanisms tend to prevent the members of various professions forming a close-knit single category of "professionals". It is chiefly by comparison with other professionals that each professional group exaggerates its own importance and deprecates its own rewards. Indeed, studies of inter-professional attitudes[39] show unexpectedly great social distance between professional groups of apparently similar status.

One group of occupations with whom the medical professional does have close relations are those other occupations who work in relation to health and illness. Such occupations as nurses, pharmacists, radiographers, occupational, speech and physiotherapists, social workers, masseurs, and clinical psychologists fall into this category. How far are these occupations professional? This question has been asked, in fact, in relation to all the above occupations and in every case the occupation itself has in various ways attempted to demonstrate its professional status. Insofar as all the occupations, along with the medical profession, perform certain tasks in relation to health and illness there seems to be no clear reason why such occupations should not be termed professions. This is particularly the case since there are few traditional tasks of healing performed by the medical professionals which are not also performed by non-medical professionals.

However, the distinction between the medical professional and the members of other occupations is that the latter's activities are derived from the former's, in that the medical professional, if not performing certain tasks, controls and has *of other H arkeo*

final responsibility for their performance. Thus, the para-professional occupations are not distinguished from the strategic professional occupations by virtue of their tasks or terminology or technology but rather by virtue of their relationship to the control over the core tasks of diagnosis and treatment. Nor is the distinction based upon the greater knowledge of the professional. In certain situations the para-professional can be in possession of a great deal of knowledge and experience by comparison with the professional. This is certainly the case with, for instance, those with specialist knowledge and training such as the pharmacist, the clinical psychologist or the radiographer. It is also the case in the relationship between the houseman and the sister. The common embarrassment and difficulty in such situations derives, in part, from the disjunction between the level of knowledge and experience on the one hand, and the line of responsibility and control on the other.

The striving for professional status by those occupations at present subordinated to the control of the strategic professions, such as medicine, may take many forms. Certain features of strategic professions, other than the crucial notion of autonomy which is outside the occupation's control, are emphasized. Practitioners may be licensed by the occupation, training may be made longer and more academic, recruitment requirements may be tightened, and codes of ethics may be produced. The development of certain features of the nursing profession illustrates such manoeuvres.[40]

The nurses' claim to be granted "professional" status has occupied a great deal of energy in many countries. Sophisticated and high level training programmes have been introduced into medical schools. Nurses in England are being encouraged by certain medical schools to take a joint nursing social science degree. Regular in-service training is arranged and encouraged, and skills other than "traditional" nursing skills, such as management, are being emphasised. There is a growing movement designed to distinguish the traditional bed-side skills, which are wholly defined by the medical profession's decision in relation to diagnostic and treatment requirements, from skills such as management which can be seen as, to an extent, independent of the traditional super-ordinate-subordinate relationship with the medical professional. The distinction extends beyond the division of tasks to a division among nursing personnel. The nursing auxiliary, the practical nurse,[41] and the general duty nurse[42] represent a subordinate occupation to the para-professional occupation of nursing. Ironically, it is the subordinate occupation which is inheriting the traditional nursing skills and tasks while the superordinate nursing occupations strive for professional status by seeking an area of autonomy in administration.[43]

Medicine as an institution of social control[44]

> The basic dilemma is that it is not within human capacity to complete the task which medical sciences impose upon themselves, but neither are we free to desist. Kahn[45]

The medical profession because of its position of legally granted and protected autonomy in relation to questions of health and illness has, by definition, become involved with, and responsible in relation to, anything to which the label illness may be attached irrespective of the professional capacity to deal with it effectively. The role of the medical professional as moral entrepeneur[46] is particularly evident in relation to those conditions or sets of behaviour which are defined as illness on the basis of their possessor's non-adherence to some notion of acceptable behaviour. To return to the example of alcoholism which has been referred to frequently, the relabelling of the drunkard as an alcoholic suffering from alcoholism, and the concomitant transfer of major interest from the church and courts to the surgery, has been managed without any demonstration that the medical profession handles the situation of the drinker or can predict outcome any more successfully than the practitioners of religion or law.

It is clear then that the importance of the fact of a particular aspect of life or set of behaviours or conditions coming under the jurisdiction of the medical profession lies not in some notion of cure but rather in relation to such ideas as individual responsibility which were discussed in Chapter IV. The implications of attaching the label illness to an increasingly wide-ranging set of conditions or actions has been termed the "medicalizing of society".[47] However ugly a term it may be, it stands for the insidious and largely undramatic process of making medicine and the labels "healthy" and "ill" relevant to an ever increasing part of human existence.

Such a development may well take place under the blanket heading of "preventive medicine". It is implicit in such a phrase that the medical profession will *treat* not only disease entities but behaviours considered to be part of a causal chain leading to the development of disease entities. Once this position is accepted by the general population then the medical profession is obliged to advise about, or intervene in relation to, any behaviour which falls into such a category. In the case of alcoholism, the medical profession would consider themselves and be considered by the general public, as relevant authorities to decide upon, for example, licensing laws or alcohol price policy if it were shown that alcohol price increases and shorter licensing hours were associated with a drop in alcohol consumption.

The idea that a time might come when a medical practitioner would decide upon the licensing hours in a particular locality should not be thought of as impossible or even extremely unlikely. For the idea that anything which is considered to affect in some way the working of the body or mind is "a medical problem" and thus within the jurisdiction of the medical profession is happily applied in other spheres. Medicine is readily seen to be a legitimate arbiter in cases of clashes of values of political principle; witness the abortion controversy. The history of the fluoridation campaigns in the United States illustrates the process clearly. Zola[48] describes it as follows:

The issue of fluoridation in the U.S. has for many years been a hot political one. It was in the political arena because in order to fluoridate local water supplies, the decision in many jurisdictions was put to a popular referendum. And when it was, it was often defeated. A solution was found and a series of State Laws were passed to make fluoridation a public health decision and to be treated as all other public health decisions, namely by the medical officers best qualified to decide questions of such technical, scientific and medical nature.

Medical professionals do not actually have to make decisions in the political or educational arena, or even lend their weight to one side or the other, for decisions to be taken in their name. For there is nothing like the phrase "for health reasons" for enhancing any proposal. The response to the "clacker" craze which swept Britain in 1971 was a fine example of the use of such a manoeuvre. In the autumn of that year thousands of children plagued their parents and schoolteachers with the awful row produced by knocking two small plastic balls together at great speed. The problem which faced school authorities was how to justify the banning of these noisy and irritating toys from school premises. There was no reasonable justification until, that is, someone reported that a number of children had broken bones in their wrists. Overnight the "irritating toys" turned into "harmful and dangerous objects" and were banned "on health grounds" from every school in several education authority areas. That other much more "harmful and dangerous" pastimes such as inter-school rugby matches should be banned as well, was not proposed.

It is not being suggested that the medical profession or the many other helping agencies are coolly-calculating empire builders plotting to take control over vast areas of late twentieth century life. What is being maintained is that the general public and legislators are placing these agencies, and the medical profession in particular, in a position in which they are expected to exercise their discretionary powers and perform decision-making functions, arguably, beyond their legitimate and willingly accepted brief.

Summary

The aim of this chapter has been to set a discussion of medicine as a profession within the wider context of the sociology of occupations. The question of occupational prestige was raised and the point was made that many occupational groups spend a great deal of time and effort making out a case for why they should be considered professional occupations.

While the difficulty of finding much agreement on what counts as being a professional was recognized, the notion of "legitimate organized autonomy"[49] was seen to be at the heart of a useful distinction between professions and other occupations. Freidson succinctly summed up the position in the following way:

> ... Unlike other occupations, professions are *deliberately* granted autonomy, including the exclusive right to determine who can legitimately do this work and how the work can be done. Virtually all occupations struggle to obtain both rights, and some manage to seize them, but only the professional is *granted* the right to exercise them legitimately.[50]

Certain aspects of medicine as a particular profession were highlighted, and the implications of legitimate organized autonomy for recruitment, education and control were outlined. The chapter ended with a short section on the relationship between professionals and para-professionals with particular attention being paid to the position of nurses and the nature of their claim and campaign for professional status. In the sphere of medicine it was seen that the para-professional was not distinguished from the professional by virtue of tasks, terminology or technology, but rather by virtue of the relationship to taken-for-granted control over and responsibility for the core tasks of diagnosis and treatment.

Suggestions for further reading:

Becker, H. S. *et al.* *Boys in White: student culture in a medical school.* University Chicago Press, Chicago, 1961.

Cogan, M. L. Toward a Definition of Professions. *Harvard Educational Review, XXIII, 33,* 1953.

Davis, F. (Ed.) *The Nursing Profession.* John Wiley and Sons, New York, 1966.

Freidson, E. *Profession of Medicine: a study of the sociology of applied knowledge.* Dodd, Mead & Co., New York, 1972.

Merton, R. K. *et al. The Student Physician.* Harvard University Press, Cambridge, 1957.

CHAPTER VI

The Hospital: a Complex Organization

"Our society is an organizational society. We are born in organizations, educated by organizations, and most of us spend much of our lives working for organizations. We spend much of our leisure time paying, playing, and praying in organizations. Most of us will die in an organization, and when the time comes for burial, the largest organization of all – the State – must grant official permission".

Etzioni[1]

For Etzioni, as the quotation shows, the notion of organization is clearly all-pervasive. But apart from it being a commonly used notion what is "an organization"? If it is of such wide generality as to be easily referred to in respect of all aspects of social life then the use of the concept might tell us everything and nothing.

Organizations: traditionally defined

Sociologists have been constructing "theories of organizations" for as long as there have been sociological theories of anything. Such theories have to a large extent been based on research in industrial settings[2] and a large proportion of them based upon a core desire to make the organizations run more smoothly and efficiently from the point of view of the management.

Two central tenets of classical organization theory[3] are, that there should be a division of labour and that this should be balanced by a unity of control. Adam Smith's description of modern manufacturing of pins in his Wealth of Nations, published in 1776, is a classical illustration of the significance of division of labour. He noted that a worker by himself might produce twenty pins a day. But by breaking down the task of making pins into its many component operations – he estimated that there were about eighteen different jobs such as straightening the wire and cutting it – Smith stated that he had seen ten workers produce 48,000 pins a day. This represented 4,800 pins per worker or 240 times what he could produce alone. The importance of unity of control, say the classic theorists, lies in the fact that the tasks have to be broken up into components by a central authority in line with a central plan of action; the efforts of each work unit need to be supervised; and the various jobs leading to the final product have to be co-ordinated.

Such a conception of organizations is only credible if it also rests upon another core assumption; namely that it is possible to identify the "goal" or "purpose" of an organization so that tasks can be delineated and controlled by reference to it. At the heart of most debates about the usefulness of one theory of organizations over another is the question of how valuable is this notion of "organizational goals".

In traditional organizational theory a "goal" is taken to be an image of some desired future state which to a greater or lesser extent may be realized. An "organizational goal" is taken to refer to a desired state of affairs which some organization, such as a school or hospital or factory, is attempting to realize. Organizations are, therefore, taken to be instruments which enable certain goals to be realized. In order to attain such goals, organizations have a formally defined structure laid down in written rules and regulations. In addition, there is the hierarchy of control and the division of labour in which each member has a prescribed task. Etzioni's definition of an organization[4] is particularly explicit about the core assumptions of such an approach.

> Organizations are social units (or human groupings) deliberately constructed and reconstructed to seek specific goals. Corporations, armies, schools, hospitals, churches and prisons are included; tribes, classes, ethnic groups, friendship groups, and families are excluded. Organizations are characterized by: (1) divisions of labour, power and communication responsi-

bilities, divisions which are not random or traditionally patterned, but deliberately planned to enhance the realization of specific goals; (2) the presence of one or more power centres which control the concerted efforts of the organization and direct them toward its goals; these power centres also must review continuously the organization's performance and re-pattern its structure, where necessary, to increase its efficiency; (3) substitution of personnel, i.e. unsatisfactory persons can be removed and others assigned their tasks. The organization can also recombine its personnel through transfer and promotion.

At first sight such an account appears very reasonable. It is quite possible to consider what we know, have experienced, or read, about hospitals, prisons, schools, factories and the like, and to see in them one or more of the features which Etzioni outlines. There is usually a division of labour, with some people doing one job and someone else doing another but related job. Certain people have more power than others, people are promoted and dismissed, and the desire to make the whole thing "more efficient" is easily recognized as being a common feature of hospitals and factories alike.

But how satisfactory is Etzioni's formulation really? Anyone who has worked in a factory or hospital will know that the everyday work of the members in it are not informed totally by the formal rules and regulations. As Smith suggests[5] there are all sorts of questions to be asked about the *actual* operation of an organization, as opposed to its diagrammatic representation on some blueprint, organizational chart, or rule book.

Does the pattern of control really work in this way? All rules and regulations need interpretation. How does this occur? Are there other 'unanticipated consequences' to planned organizational change? How do informal communications affect the . . . structure?

The orthodox formulation of what an organization is, can be shown to be deficient in a crucial aspect by again referring to the core notion of "organizational goal". Even the briefest acquaintance with a hospital, university or factory will reveal that even in their most formal statements organizations rarely admit only one goal. Members of a university would readily admit that it is geared to research as well as to teaching, a hospital to the advancement of knowledge as well as to relieving the suffering of patients and a prison to the reform of the inmates as well as the protection of those outside its walls. Such multiple goals or purposes may be to a greater or lesser extent complementary. But even when complementary, they give rise to conflict over approach and means.

It may be that the members of an organization would formally acknowledge that it was geared to the pursuit of one goal, but it is likely that the goal would either be of such diffuseness as to be indefinable, or of such generality as to be equally well applied to almost all organizations. Thus, to say that the goal of a school is "learning" in no way enables us to distinguish a school from a university, a teaching hospital, or a factory with apprentices in it. Similarly, it will not help us to understand the differences between the particular organization, way of working, and attitudes of members, of particular schools. Thus, such a diffuse goal does not help us to distinguish between types of organization or to understand what is going on in any one organization.

Up to now we have assumed that, while there may be drawbacks to thinking of organizations as having one goal, there may be some value in thinking of multiple goals for an organization which all members would acknowledge and accept. But again, this notion is difficult to maintain. Studies of industries,[6] churches,[7] police forces,[8] and voluntary organizations,[9] among many, have shown how the members of organizations define the goals of those organizations in a whole variety of often quite incompatible ways.

Another major defect of much traditional writing is that it has tended to consider a particular organization in isolation from the environmental context in which it is placed. Thus, ideas about goals and practice have been considered in isolation from the ideas and beliefs which inform members of the organizations in their activities outside those organizations. In Chapter I, when the notion of social group was being discussed it was pointed out that any attempt to understand social action in, for example, a particular illness situation must take account of those other groups to which the actors belong, what values and beliefs inform their behaviour in those groups, what demands are made on them, how compatible are their self-defined goals in relation to one group with their goals in relation to the illness situation, and so on. For sociology, if it does anything, draws attention to the many social positions which are occupied by any one person and attempts to indicate the implications of this fact for social action in particular situations. Unfortunately, much organizational theory has tended to explain action in particular organizational settings purely by reference to organizational factors. In other words, a lack of interest has been shown in the impingement of expectations in relation to the occupancy of non-organizational social positions upon the definition of appropriate behaviour associated with organizational social positions.

Silverman[10] outlines certain key features of five leading schools of organizational analysis—Human Relations,[11] Organizational Psychology,[12] Socio-Technical Systems,[13] Structural-Functionalism,[14] and Decision-Making Theory.[15] Taken as a whole they represent the way in which organizations have traditionally been analysed. Further, they form the basic material for those who, in particular organizations, have been in a position to alter working conditions or everyday practices. All these approaches tend to be founded upon the notion of the goals of an organization and have then gone on to analyse the function certain factors perform for these goals. Unfortunately, such an approach carries with it implications that organizations are in some sense independent of the definitions and purposes of their members. This is, of course, the crucial weakness of the approach.

Where the definitions and purposes of members of organizations have been taken into account, the orthodox theories have usually identified only the interests of one group. In industrial setting this has been management, rather than workers on the shop floor, in hospitals or prison settings this has been the interests of the staff rather than the patients or the prisoners. As a result of such an approach the guiding principle informing the investigation has been to analyse situations so that such analyses could aid the solution of certain "problems" as defined by the "higher participants".[16]

Thus, such organizational theories have taken the problems of the manager, just as by and large educational and medical sociologists have taken the problems of the teacher or the professional, and, accepting his assumptions, offered explanations for some discrepancy between the professional's beliefs about what ought to be and what he sees to be, in fact, the case. As the sociologist of education tried to explain why some children "failed that" or "went unwillingly to" school, so the industrial sociologist attempted to explain why "job satisfaction was low" on a particular assembly line, and the medical sociologist why cancer patients "delayed in seeking treatment". The implicit assumption was that dropping out of the formal educational system counted as failure, that children ought to go willingly to school, that workers on an assembly line should gain satisfaction from their job, and that people should consult professional medical authorities about suspected cancer. The sociologists had not only, in Seeley's[17] terms, "taken" rather than "made" the problems to which they addressed themselves, but had also taken the managers'/teachers'/professionals' assumptions about ultimate goals and values in terms of which problems were identified, explanations sought, and "solutions" offered.

In sum, then, the orthodox organizational theorists do not present a picture of real organizations but, as Albrow argues,[18] only a hypothetical or ideological future situation.

> In a situation where the members of an organization disagree as to what constitutes the organizational goal, the requirements of the orthodox definition can severely prejudice an objective account. At its worst the . . . determination to impute clear cut goals can lead to a point where . . . one is actually siding with one party or another in saying what the objectives ought to be.

Organizations: a more realistic approach

In order to avoid the crucial bias of the orthodox theories of organization Albrow[19] suggests the following definitions of organizations as:

> ... social units where individuals are conscious of their membership and legitimize their co-operative activities primarily by reference to the attainment of impersonal goals rather than moral standards.

Such a formulation retains the important notion of goal attainment but avoids the assumption that goals are unitary, specific, stable, or the prerogative of one group's definition. It thus becomes vital for any understanding of social action in any particular organization to appreciate the varying definitions of the situation held by the actors, and their varying purposes.

The importance of attempting to understand the differing perspectives in terms of which different actors in any situation interpret the social world about them has been stressed throughout this book. Sociologists attach a great deal of importance to this notion of "the definition of the situation". The most familiar formulation is to be found in the work of the early American sociologist W. I. Thomas who held that:

> ... preliminary to any self-determined act of behaviour there is always a stage of examination and deliberation which we call the *definition of the situation*.[20]

As a corollary, Thomas later postulated that "if men define situations as real, they are in their consequences".[21] The implications of such a stance is that social actors engage in the construction of reality[22] and engage in action on a basis of a continual process of constructing order out of the multiple options that seem to be available. In respect of organizations, sociologists are not saying that each situation is to be defined anew and in a vacuum. Again, as was pointed out in Chapter I, social action in any particular situation is constrained by what ideas happen to be available to the actors involved, which will in part determine what they *choose* to do, and by what conditions actually face them and under which they act, which will in part determine what they are *able* to do.

From such a perspective, it is clear that organizational rules are in essence created by the interaction of participants in the course of their everyday work in the organization. This again conflicts with the assumptions of orthodox theories which tend to conceptualize organizational rules as decided upon and structured – the rules may be bent or ignored but such action constitutes deviant cases. The weakness of such a position is that it assumes that the way in which men actually organize their activities in organizations is somehow less real than the set of guide lines sanctified in formal codes of ethics, organizational charts or rule books. On the contrary, it is the negotiated, informal guide-lines to conduct which have the greater reality to those whose conduct they guide. The informal, negotiated rules give meanings in terms in which the participants actually experience the situation; they are their "definition of the situation". The official rules, on the other hand, may rarely be experienced as immediate and direct constraints to action. Indeed, we need only think of what "working to rule" by railway men, teachers, or people in the gas industry for example, has meant to appreciate the distinction between formal rules and everyday activity. But while there is a distinction between formal rules and guides to everyday conduct it should not be imagined that even formal rule-books are "disembodied standards".[23] Such formal rules did not just arrive on the scene, they were human creations just like informal guides to conduct. The rules themselves are usually informal guides operating at a particular time which have become crystallized by their codification. Thus, even the formal rules are negotiated. The idea of organizations as negotiated rather than preordained orders is succinctly presented in the following extended quotation from Strauss[24]:

Rules are not disembodied standards. Like other negotiable products, they are human arrangements. In large-scale organizations, they tend to be written down, codified and specifically sanctioned. . . . But the assumption that rules (or values) stand outside negotiable realms assumes a consistency of conduct that surely exists only in the eye of the beholding theorist.

When one asks actors why they have acted as they have or what rules obtained, neat answers are sometimes forthcoming. Whether one asks them directly or simply adduces their answers – from observations or oblique interviews — one is seeking their grounds for action . . . but one man's grounds may not be the grounds of another. It is only when all agree that the grounds for action are "the rule" that consensus obtains . . . Once the parties disagree, negotiation becomes explicit, sometimes ending in actual formal revision of the rule.

Clearly the sociologist must examine the rules within a rhetorical framework. Rules enter into current and future conduct in that actors define rules as relevant to situations, which means that they must define situations as related or unrelated to specific governing rules. Consequently, . . . people expect rules to control their own and others behaviour. They also counter other's claims to be rule-appliers with claims of their own.

Certain implications of such a perspective for those who work in, or study, or are referred as patients to, or in some way participate in those organizations known as hospitals, are discussed in the remainder of the chapter.

The hospital

"It Defies All Logic – But A Hospital Does Function." Title of an article by *Mauksch*.[25]

The literature on hospitals as a particular type of organization is vast. Similarly, the particular perspectives taken by the authors have included looking at the hospital from the point of view of managerial control,[26] or from the point of view of a process system.[27] Other studies concentrate more upon human resources,[28] or looking at the hospital from the specific vantage point of some participating occupation such as the doctor,[29] the nurse[30] the administrator,[31] and others.[32] Still others have been concerned with the activities and attitudes of the patient.[33]

Whatever else it may be, the hospital is an organization in which various categories of people, who will all have their own priorities and particular perspectives, come together as participants in some health-related activity. Just as the hospital is a primary work place for those involved in the care and cure of the sick, so it has also become the primary context for the training of medical personnel of various types and for medical research. Given all this, is it possible, as orthodox organizational theorists would have us believe, to define *the* goal in relation to which the complex range of activities are "planned, deliberately structured" and "constantly and self-consciously"[34] structured and re-structured?

Only a brief acquaintance as a participant in a hospital is sufficient to show that such a simple view of organizations bears so little relationship to the everyday world of the hospital as to be of little value as an explanatory device. This is so because, as Strauss puts it[35]

> . . . no one knows what the hospital "is" on any given day unless he has a comprehensive grasp of the combination of rules, policies, agreements, understandings, facts, contracts and other working arrangements that currently obtain. In a pragmatic sense, that combination "is" the hospital at that moment, its social order.

Any changes which impinge upon that current everyday order

> . . . whether ordinary change, like the introduction of a new staff member or a betrayed contract, or unusual changes, like the introduction of a new technology or new theory – will necessitate re-negotiation or re-appraisal. . . .

Thus, there will be a new order.

> Not merely the re-establishment of an old order or re-institution
> of a previous equilibrium.

However, while having emphasised the essentially negotiated order of hospital organization this is not to say, of course, that there are not structural features which most hospitals "as hospitals" share. Thus, it is not impossible to talk about certain common features of hospitals and certain common problems experienced by particular categories of participants in hospitals. While the idea of "the organizational goal" of hospitals has been discarded as unhelpful, it is still possible to identify and describe the nature and implications of dominant group policies of particular hospitals or sets of hospitals. In a study of voluntary general hospitals in America, Perrow[36] has shown how such dominant policies change over time depending upon the controlling power of different interest groups.

At first, the hospitals were dominated by trustees who administered the finances upon which the hospital depended. At this stage the hospitals were primarily used as instruments of social philanthropy. In the second stage, as a result of increasing technical complexity, medical staff dominated hospital policy. Here emphasis was placed on high technical quality, particularly in teaching and research. In such a situation, the roles of teaching and research in a hospital may well conflict with those of individual patient care if major resources are devoted to areas of research simply because they are prestigious in the eyes of the scientific community. This has been the basis of much recent comment on developments in heart transplant surgery. In the third stage, as a result of increasing administrative complexity, professional administrators came to dominate hospital policy. In this stage operative policy stressed financial solvency, administrative efficiency and a cautious approach to such new forms of care as intensive therapy units or home care programmes.

While trustees are not an important part of the British

hospital system the relationship between medical and administrative participants is a constant feature of the negotiated order of the hospital. The nature of the relationship in any particular hospital has widespread implications.

In an article entitled "Two lines of authority are one too many" Smith[37] discusses one obvious feature of hospitals which distinguishes it from the archetypal organization identified in orthodox theories, namely the fact that in hospitals there is not just one line of formal authority. There is the authority of the professional based, as was pointed out in the previous chapter, upon his granted and protected autonomy, on the one hand, and the formal administrative authority, on the other. This complex of both professional and bureaucratic authority makes the hospital a quite different type of work place from the factory. The difference has clear implications for all concerned. For example, as Freidson[38] puts it:

> Unlike the foreman, who is caught "in the middle" between his legitimate superiors and subordinates, the nurse is caught between two superiors, administrative and medical. The latter is not her bureaucratic superior, that is to say, while the floor nurse is subject to the orders of her supervisor, who is her official superior in the hospital hierarchy, she is also subject to the orders of the physician involved in the care of her patients by virtue of his superior knowledge and responsibility. Similarly, justifying his demands to the well-being of his patient, the physician can and does give "orders" to other hospital personnel even though he is not a bureaucratically defined superior.

The medical professional is able to intervene in many places in the hospital and justify his intervention on the basis of a "medical emergency"—a situation in which the well-being of a patient is said to be seriously in jeopardy and in which it is the professional alone who knows what needs to be done.[39] But while the professional, the administrator and others may differ in their assessment of the legitimacy of the claim to resources on the basis of "emergency" the professional's definition will generally prevail. However, the setting up of emergency admissions committees in American hospitals to review the justification of suspending ordinary procedures and priorities suggests that the definition by one professional of a "medical emergency" may not be shared by his colleagues who also seek control over scarce organizational resources and facilities. But the fact that the emergency admissions committees are composed of professionals again confirms the points made in the last chapter about medicine being an autonomous occupation, in that it alone evaluates the work and judgment of its own members.

The hospital is characterized by built-in conflict between essentially incompatible bureacratic and professional authority. Bureaucracy assumes a hierarchy of power in which the higher in rank have more power than the lower ones and can control and co-ordinate the latter's activities. Such hierarchies in hospitals may be symbolically expressed in styles of dress. Cohen[40] comments that:

> In the nursing world uniform denotes rank with subtler nuance than in the army. Serjeants only bear an extra stripe. Sisters rejoice in frillier caps, bunchier skirts, more buttons and longer sleeves.

By contrast, the professional is basically responsible to his conscience. The ultimate justification for a professional act is that it is, to the best of the professional's knowledge, the right act. He might consult his colleagues before he acts, but the decision is his. If he errs, he will still be defended by his peers. The defence will, in all likelihood, not be made by reference to the correctness of the professional's compliance with particular orders but rather in terms of his right to exercise judgment in particular situations.

The fact that the professional's conduct will be judged by his peers again reminds us, if such were needed, that the hospital is not a closed system but comprised of various categories of persons for whom the hospital setting and its everyday practices form a greater or lesser part of their lives.

For just as participants occupy particular positions *vis-à-vis* others within the organization so they occupy positions in other settings where their activities are informed by the world of the hospital and vice versa. The place of the hospital in relation to other formal medical organizations, settings and facilities will be briefly discussed in the next chapter, but whatever else it is the hospital is clearly a major work setting for medical practice.

The general practitioner who does not supervise the care of his patients in hospital loses them on hospitalization. In a medical system where a fee-for-service situation operates he may not regain their custom. In Britain where patients tend to be registered with general practitioners and where there is a separation between hospital and general practice which prevents the general practitioner from caring for his patient in hospital but also discourages his patient from obtaining primary medical care from a hospital, he may lose his patient on hospitalization but is more or less assured of regaining him on discharge. Again then, any attempt to understand the operation of a hospital, or the action of particular people in particular ward situations, or the characteristics of patients or practitioners in a hospital, needs to be informed by a consideration of the medical and social context in which the hospital is set. However, some hospitals are more independent, and have a more enclosed system, than others. Long-term mental hospitals clearly have features which encourage people to speak of them "as if" they were totally independent institutions.

While no organization is, of course, completely isolated the idea of a "total institution"[41] has been used to apply to a category of organizations which appear to share certain features. Institutions such as mental hospitals, army barracks, prisons, old people's homes, and boarding schools have been taken to represent organizations which, to a greater extent than other organizations, have a distinctive culture which is largely isolated from the cultural and social setting of its environment. The central features of "total institutions" are the bringing together of groups of co-participants who live their lives in one place – thus breaking down the barriers usually separating different spheres of life – and under one authority which organizes the different features of life within an over-all plan. Goffman describes some details as follows:

> First, all aspects of life are conducted in the same place and under the same single authority. Second, each phase of the member's daily activity is carried on in the immediate company of a large batch of others, all of whom are treated alike and are required to do the same things together. Third, all phases of the day's activities are tightly scheduled, with one activity leading at a prearranged time to the next, the whole sequence of activities being imposed from above by a system of explicit formal rulings and a body of officials. Finally, the various enforced activities are brought together into a single rational plan purportedly designed to fulfil the official aims of the institution.[42]

It is not surprising that in organizations which, if only loosely, approximate to Goffman's outline those who participate in them should, as Wing[43] points out in relation to schizophrenics, appear apathetic about life outside. However, such "institutionalism" is not only a characteristic of the lower participants in such organizations such as patients, prisoners or schoolboys. The inability of staff members whether charge nurses, warders, or housemasters to face or adjust to life outside the institutions is a less well documented phenomenon but no less real.

The "problem" of communication

> It is quite clear that the widely held view that communications between hospital staff and patients are in need of improvement is amply justified by the evidence. *Ley and Spelman.*[44]

The amount of research work carried out in the area of communication between hospital staff and their patients is immense. A short and clear presentation of much of this evidence is contained in the book by Ley and Spelman entitled "Communicating with the Patient",[45] while a more theoretical, wide-ranging discussion, "The communication of information about illness" by Waitzkin and Stoeckle,[46] identifies certain "clinical, sociological and methodological considerations". By and large, the core problems to which the majority of the work is addressed are "how can the information which the doctor wants be better got from the patient?", "how can the information and advice the doctor wants the patient to receive be got across more satisfactorily?", and "how can patients' dissatisfaction with the quality and amount of information they receive be reduced?"

Ley and Spelman clearly demonstrate that the transmission of information in hospital is not only a question of goodwill. For even where there was a whole hearted desire on the part of the staff to provide and give information other barriers were found to exist.

> They include misconceptions and ignorance of the nature of various illnesses on the part of the patient, and their diffidence when confronted by doctors and hospital staff. This diffidence makes them fail to ask for clarification of obscurities in what the doctor has said to them. This, combined with misconceptions about illness, means that often, when a doctor tells a patient something, the patient will either not understand, or understand something quite different from what the doctor intended.[47]

For communication of information to be effective, then, hospital staff should have a good idea of what medical knowledge patients possess. This is no easy task. The review also stressed the obvious, but often overlooked, point that if the communication of instructions or advice about treatment is to be effective the patient needs to remember it. Ley and Spelman suggest that:

1. Patients forget much of what the doctor tells them.
2. Instructions and advice are more likely to be forgotten than other information.
3. The more a patient is told the greater the proportion he will forget.
4. Patients will remember best: (*a*) what they are told first; (*b*) what they consider most important.
5. Intelligent patients do not remember more than less intelligent ones.
6. Older patients remember just as much as younger ones.
7. Moderately anxious patients recall more of what they are told than highly anxious patients and patients who are not anxious.
8. The more medical knowledge a patient has the more he will recall.
9. If the patient writes down what the doctor says he will remember it just as well as if he merely hears it.

These findings, say the authors, suggest a number of obvious remedies for seeing that patients remember what they are told.

1. Make the patient write down what he is told. He will then have a record to consult.
2. When giving information to patients give the most important information first.
3. If advice or instructions are given, emphasize their importance.

Given the binding simplicity of these recommendations, it is surprising that there is such a thing as a communication "problem" in hospitals at all. The reason that there *is* such a problem is due, of course, to the fact that information, its creation, its handling and the various perceptions people have of its usefulness and adequacy, are rather more complex matters than such an analysis appears to suggest.

The first point to make is that the potential value of the majority of work on communications in hospital is undermined at the outset by making the assumption, as Ley and Spelman do, that communication is something which staff somehow *do* with patients, but not patients with staff. The majority of problems identified in the literature are associated with the impediments to the transmission of information from the staff member to the patient. It is significant that Ley and Spelman's book is called "Communicating with the Patient" and not "Communicating with the Doctor". In the few cases where the information which the patient transmits is identified as important it is usually deemed important only in so far as it is a resource for the professional. A perceptive statement of this position is made by Bird[48] when he says that the main object of talking to the patient is:

> . . . to get the patient to talk, to hear from him, to listen. To find out not only about his immediate symptoms but about him – his strengths and his weaknesses, his experiences through life and his reaction to them.

For to learn only about the immediate causes of illness

> . . . is to learn only the final steps in the history of disease. Admittedly this is the urgent thing to do, and it is also the easiest, but in most illnesses it is no more than elaborate first aid and not of lasting importance.

The clinical importance of history taking is linked by Waitzkin and Stoeckle to the transmission of information by the clinician. Their point is slightly different from Bird's in that they draw attention to the fact that:

> The patient's ability to provide a meaningful history depends largely on his understanding of prior experience with illness.

Part of the lack of adequate information from the patient, hey point out,

> . . . results from the patient's imperfect memory or comprehension. However, previous information from the doctor that is incomplete, erroneous, or contradictory also limits the accuracy of a history at a later point in time.

Therefore, the hospital staff's success in transmitting information about illness "... feeds back ... through the patient's later ability or inability to provide a meaningful history".

Here again, the purpose of the transmission of information by the doctor to the patient is seen to be its value *for the professional* at a later date. It is not being suggested, of course, that such a process is not of value to the patient as well. Clearly, the more accurate the history is the more competently will the professional be likely to perform his service for the patient. The value to both professional and layman of supplying more detailed information to the patient with accuracy and consistency was clearly recognized by both the Medical Defence Union and the Royal College of Nursing who, in 1961, produced a "Memorandom on steps that might be taken to obviate the risk of an operation being performed on the wrong patient, side, limb or digit".[49]

However, if "the problem of communication" in hospital is to be understood and explained, the satisfactoriness of communication should not be judged solely in terms of the convenience or demands of the professional and his clinical practice and only incidentally in terms of the patient's satisfaction insofar as it furthers those professional ends. It is quite possible to study the communications system of the hospital, or any other medical setting, in terms of how far information exchange better enables the patient to, for instance, maintain what he perceives as satisfactory relationships outside the hospital and only incidentally in terms of the professional's convenience or satisfaction insofar as it furthers the layman's ends. The point is, that it is quite possible to keep analytically separate the "problem" of communication as defined by the professional, from the "problem" of communication as defined by the patient. A realistic study of communication and information in hospitals needs to keep both these questions firmly in mind.

Satisfaction with in-hospital information

Patients' dissatisfaction with in-hospital communication is a constantly recorded phenomenon.[50] But just as the communication between staff and the patient is a matter of concern so is the communication between staff and the patient's family. This is particularly important where the patient is a child when adequate exchanges of information have clear implications for the well-being of the child. Just as it is important for the doctor to talk to adult patients so it is important for him to talk to the parents of child patients since it is usually the best way of obtaining full details of the child's medical history.

Hospital staff often make a practice of not telling patients about their illness and its treatment in the belief that it might confuse or worry them and so make the situation even worse. This can happen. But there is also ample evidence that not telling the patient about his illness may have an even more disturbing effect. [51]

As far as parents are concerned, Skipper [52] provides evidence to suggest that mothers who are given a lot of information about their children's hospitalization and surgery suffer less distress than other mothers over the event and are better able to adapt to the hospital experience. Elsewhere it has been suggested [53] that when mothers are very worried about hospital experience this has implications at two levels for the well-being of their child patients. First, following Escalona's notion of "contagion", [54] as a direct result of the anxiety itself and secondly, as a result of the mothers' behaviour in response to that anxiety. Mothers who are worried tend to visit their children less, to be less likely to prepare their children for hospitalization, and generally to try to avoid the facts and personnel of the hospital situation.

In the case of child patients, therefore, satisfactory in-hospital communication between parents and medical staff is important for the effective diagnosis and treatment of the child, for the parents' adaptation to the hospital situation and, as a result of both, for the well-being of the child itself.

In a study of parental attitudes and behaviour in relation to the hospitalization of their young children, [55] the parents satisfaction with in-hospital information they received about their children was one of the points of interest. The particular points which are now made about this study can be extended to adult patient-staff communication. The problems are merely exaggerated when the patient is a child since the exchange of information about the patient is two-step.

Satisfactory in-patient information was defined, purely and simply, as information with which mothers were reported as being satisfied. No comment was, or could be, made about the hospital's efforts to provide parents of young children with authoritative information. The particular questions on the questionnaire concerning information were :

1a. When X (the child) was in hospital were you able to find out all you wanted to know about his/her condition?
1b. If 'yes' to 1a. Who from?.........................
1c. If 'no' to 1a.
   i. What would you like to have been told about?......................
   ii. Anything else?..
   iii. Did you ask anyone about this?.......................................
   iv. If 'yes' to iii:
      Who did you ask?...
   v. What was their reply?...

Just over a third of the mothers interviewed said that they did not receive sufficient information. Three preliminary points can be made about this; first, it is possible that no-one was *able* to provide the information that was wanted. For example, if a diagnosis is uncertain it is impossible for anyone to give a satisfactory answer to a mother who wants to know *exactly* what is wrong with her child or *exactly* how long he is to be in hospital. As has been pointed out before, one of the constraints upon social action is that which restricts what the actor is *able* to do.

Since there is a great deal of uncertainty in the treatment of illness and disease a medical practitioner might restrict communication with patients, or their parents, to protect himself from admitting either that he is uncertain, or committing himself, on insufficient evidence, to a diagnosis or course of treatment which he might subsequently have to change.[56] Keeping patients uninformed also allows nurses to protect themselves. "If a patient is not informed about his care and treatment", says Skipper "he is hampered in evaluating whether the nurses are performing their duties adequately". This highlights the other main framework within which social action can be considered, namely the ideas about appropriate behaviour which in part determine from among the things he is *able* to do, what the actor will in fact *choose* to do.

The second reason why some mothers may not have received as much information as they would have liked about their children is simply a matter of physical distance. Wesen [58] suggests that important restrictions on in-hospital communications have accompanied the change from large open wards to small wards and cubicle systems. A cubicle restricts not only the satisfaction of the patient's need for contact with other people, but also his desire to secure information about his illness, technical medical procedures and the general social organization of the hospital. When it is parents of child patients, essentially outsiders, who are seeking information they, like patients in cubicles, are cut off from any kind of involvement in ward affairs. They are likely to want even more communication with the staff than the adult in-patient, since parents have no opportunity to obtain information from other in-patients in a childrens' ward. In addition, parents are seldom able to watch the nurses working with their child patients since staff often disappear from the ward during visiting time.[59]

A further barrier to obtaining authoritative information is the patients' and visitors' impression of the medical and nursing staff as constantly overworked and performing very urgent, if not life saving, acts. The feeling of being afraid to take up the staff's valuable time is very real[60] in spite of the fact that, especially in children's wards, there is often very little technical nursing to be done.[61] If, as Cartwright suggests,[62] social distance between patients and doctors contributes to a feeling of awe with which patients regard the doctors, then we would expect mothers whose husbands had manual occupations, to have been less likely to have received any of their information from doctors. This was the case. In addition, these mothers were less likely to have spoken to the doctor in charge of their child's case, and less likely also to have known the surgeon's name if their child had to have an operation. Moreover, these differences between the non-manual and manual groups cannot be explained in terms of the difference in the amount of importance attached to speaking to the doctor in charge, since, when asked, 90 per cent of both groups said that it was important to do so.

Just as the mothers whose husbands had manual occupations were less ready than other mothers to approach the doctor for information so the doctor may be less ready to speak to them. In addition to there being a tendency to underestimate the ability of this group to understand what is being said to them. Doctors, who come from different socio-cultural backgrounds, may feel that they get little personal satisfaction from interaction with manual groups.[63]

If social distance and other factors mentioned are to account for the manual group having less contact with doctors, and this in turn to account for their lower level of satisfaction with in-hospital information, we are assuming that doctors, as opposed to members of the nursing staff, are the most satisfactory source of information. This again was clearly the case. While 89 per cent of contacts with the doctor resulted in the patient being "satisfied", 76 per cent of contacts with sisters so resulted, and only 25 per cent of contacts with nurses.

It must be stressed again that this material refers only to the mothers' *reports* of being satisfied, and says nothing of the quality of the information offered. But for whatever reason this is a particularly unfortunate state of affairs since junior nursing staff are often the only people with whom visitors come into contact.[64] However, when nurses could not or did not feel in a position to answer questions and quite properly advised mothers to speak either to the sister or the doctor in charge, the barriers of social and physical distance, time, and the fear of being a nuisance or asking what might appear to be a stupid question prevented mothers from doing so.

A further reason why nurses tend to be less satisfactory sources of in-hospital information is that for them, unlike doctors, the information process is likely to be just one-way. Nurses seldom have cause to talk to patients, or their parents, in order to get information to help them to make decisions about diagnoses or courses of treatment. Since the returns for the nurse are negligible, she may keep communication with patients, or their parents, as functionally specific and instrumental as possible. This, in turn, will tend to limit the kind of opportunity with which patients and their parents need in order to ask for the information they want.

Questionnaire based studies

This study of the "problem" of parents' satisfaction with in-hospital information about their young children has been discussed at length for two main reasons. First, in order to emphasise the wide ranging and complex issues involved in the question of communication, but also to indicate some of the grave limitations of this kind of study. How satisfactory is it to base a discussion of in-hospital communication on a retrospective questionnaire study? In other words, how much does it aid our understanding of the practical issues involved in the exchange and control of information to ask questions of one party to the communication at some time after the event?

An alternative way of approaching the question of studying behaviour in illness situations, by being either a known or unknown observer, is discussed in the next chapter. But having referred to a questionnaire study of attitudes and opinions this is possibly the best place to briefly consider the major strengths and weaknesses of such an approach. The use of questionnaires is particularly widespread. Unfortunately, as Oppenheim in his book "Questionnaire Design and Attitude Measurements" says[65]:

> Survey literature abounds with portentious conclusions based
> on faulty inferences from insufficient evidence wrongly as-
> sembled and misguidedly collected.

Obviously there are problems, the range and complexity of which cannot be done justice to here.[66]

Some of the problems associated with sampling and representativeness were discussed in Chapter II in connection with health surveys. But if we turn from such essentially descriptive questions as how many people have breast cancer, or how many people say they would vote conservative if there was a general election tomorrow, to a consideration of social relationships in particular settings then limitations of the questionnaire approach are immediately revealed.

The strength of the questionnaire is that it enables the same form of words to be presented to several people. It enables a researcher, with the aid of a number of helpers, to obtain the opinions or reports of a large number of people very quickly. It enables very specific questions to be asked and measurements made, which can be related to particular discussions and enable certain conclusions to be drawn. In sum, as Oppenheim puts it[67] "survey design as a whole is aimed at precision, logic, tightness and efficiency". Its value to traditional epidemiological enquiry has been considerable.[68]

But, there are limitations. At a technical level there are many possible sources of error.[69]

> Sampling errors; errors due to non-response; bias due to
> questionnaire-design and question-wording; unreliability or
> lack of validity of various techniques used; varieties of inter-
> viewer bias; respondent unreliability, ignorance, misunder-
> standing, reticence or bias; bias in recording and coding the
> responses; errors in processing and statistical analysis; faults in
> interpretation of results. Great strides have been made in
> recent years in the improvement of sampling methods and the
> assessment of sampling-error limits, but the remaining sources
> of error are still very much with us, and any of them could
> easily outweigh the gains from improved sampling techniques.

Nor is this all, for each of these sources of error covers a dozen
or more types of error, to each of which a chapter could be
devoted.

Even more fundamental, in relation to the problem of studying
social action, is the fact that questionnaire studies are geared
to the investigation of individuals. Not only this but they are
geared to the questioning of individuals out of the context in
relation to which questions are being asked. Thus, any
questionnaire study concerned with, for example, communication between hospital staff and the parents of young child
patients must, by definition, be conducted outside the
particular hospital context in question. The questions must
either refer to some time in the past with all the problems of
recall that such an exercise entails, or with some hypothetical
future situation, with all the difficulties which are entailed in
that. In fact, the only situation which can be directly referred
to by respondents in a questionnaire study is "completing a
questionnaire"!

The crucial problem with questionnaire studies which are
used in the course of some attempt to explain social action is
that *social* action, as has been stressed throughout this book,
is "action oriented towards the past, present or expected
future behaviour of others".[70] In other words, *social* action is
situationally defined and can only be understood in these
terms. It is the inter-relation between various people occupying
positions in particular social situations which is the stuff of
social life and which the sociologist is at pains to attempt to
understand, describe and indicate the implications of. Clearly,
to ask questions of individuals, out of context, is not likely to
advance such an enterprise very far. Just as in the process of
diagnosis the clinician's inquiries are informed by what he
knows of the past history of his patient, the information he
receives from others involved, the reports of his colleagues and
the nuances which he perceives through clinical experience,
so the sociologist, if he is to explain *social* interaction in medical
situations, must rely on something other than replies to

questions asked of individuals outside those situations. The role of the sociologist *in* the particular situations in which he is interested is discussed in the next chapter.

Just as the actions of individuals cannot be understood outside the social context in which they are set, so medical practice in one organization, such as the hospital, cannot be adequately understood without considering the place of that organization in relation to other organizations and types of activity concerned with the provision of medical care. This is also discussed in the next chapter.

Summary

This chapter has concentrated attention upon one of the common work-places of medical practice – the hospital. The notion of the hospital as a complex organization was discussed, aspects of various theories of organizations were outlined, and the extent and nature of their relevance for gaining some understanding of the everyday world of the hospital, was indicated.

Features of medical organizational theory were discussed and, in particular, the importance for such theories of the core notion of an organizational goal were stressed. However, these theories were seen to be deficient in certain crucial aspects, for instance in their tendency to consider particular organizations in isolation from the environmental context in which they were set, and the common assumption that the definition of "efficiency" and "problems" was the prerogative of the "higher participants".

The importance was stressed of an approach which acknowledges and is built upon the fact that all participants in any organization have their own definitions of the situation which may be shared to a greater or lesser extent. From such a perspective it is clear that organizational rules are, in essence, creations of the interaction of participants in the course of their everyday work in the organization. Hospitals, as particular organizations, were seen to be characterized by the existence

of two different types of authority – bureaucratic and professional – and by a constantly referred to "problem" of communication. In the light of consideration of a study of
satisfaction with in-hospital information the central weakness
of a questionnaire approach to the study of social action was
identified.

Suggestions for further reading:

Coser, R. L. *Life in the Ward*. Michigan State University Press,
Michigan, 1962.

Freidson, E. *The Hospital in Modern Society*. Free Press, New
York, 1963.

Goffman, E. *Asylums*. Anchor Books, Doubleday, New York,
1961.

Ley, P. and Spelman, *Communicating with the Patient*. Staples
Press, London, 1967.

Silverman, D. *Theory of Organizations*. Heinemann, London,
1970.

CHAPTER VII

Sociology and the Provision of Medical Care

"One of the reasons why it is difficult to generalise about the effectiveness of the National Health Service is because it is, of course, not the monolithic organisation which it is sometimes regarded as being. The Service comprises a large number of activities many of which are in a continuous process of change, reflecting the moods and development of society itself."

McLachlan[1]

Most of this short book has focused upon circumscribed and to an extent manageable problems. Specific areas of concern have been parcelled out and some of the sociologist's interests in relation to each have been presented. But a consideration of "becoming ill" cannot be completely separated from a consideration of "being a patient", any more than a consideration of "the patient and the doctor" can be separated from that of "medicine as a profession". In just the same way the analysis of "the hospital as a complex organization" cannot be divorced from a consideration of all the other organizations, agencies and activities which constitute the framework for the provision of medical care.

Inter-relatedness of medical activities

The whole complex of interrelated medical activities are not organized to fit some overall plan of action. The organization of particular types of medical, other professional, social work, local authority, and voluntary, activity has developed over a considerable time in response to changes in technology and morbidity, the demand of particular interests, and "the needs of society" as defined by people with sufficient power to translate their particular visions into reality. It is hardly surprising, therefore, that the precise form in which the provision of medical care is organized should vary from place to place and be "in a continuous process of change".[2]

In order to understand why a particular form of medical care is as it is in any particular setting it is necessary to trace the development of interrelated ideas and practices. To discuss the natures of such histories is clearly well beyond the scope of this little book. But as an antidote to those accounts of medical history which merely document events related to the development of those aspects of medical care which are considered important today, and ignore the history and development of unhelpful, outmoded, or false medical conventions, Sigerist's History of Medicine[3] is an acknowledged masterpiece. For illuminating accounts of the growth of particular medical practices and organizations in the history of everyday medical work one can consult, for example, Bullough[4] on the term "doctor", and Rosen or Abel-Smith on hospitals.[6]

But just as present day medicine is the result of various intellectual, organizational and personal interests, so the provision of medical care is a complex of inter-related activities conducted by people with a whole range of primary interests, orientations and perspectives. Other books present detailed descriptions of the different occupations and services involved in medical care,[6] their administrative structure,[7] and the statutory relations of one organization with another.[8] The remainder of this book is concerned with the relationship between sociology and the provision of medical care.

A number of years ago Robert Straus[9] suggested that medical sociology can be logically divided into two concerns – sociology *in* medicine and the sociology *of* medicine. The former, he argued, was concerned with collaborative research or teaching with medical scientists and the attempt at integration of concepts and techniques. The latter, he saw to be concerned with the study of such factors as organizational structure, role relationships, the functions of medicine as a system of behaviour and similar issues. In other words he saw sociology *in* medicine as being geared towards the development of medical science and practice, and to the solution of "problems" defined as such by medical practitioners, while he saw the sociology *of* medicine as the attempt to solve sociological problems in medical settings.

Straus observed that these two types of medical sociology appeared to be incompatible and he indicated that he felt that the sociology *of* medicine could be carried out best by persons outside the formal medical settings who did not become too closely identified with medical teaching or clinical research. Unfortunately, such a position is undermined by one basic and crucial fact concerning the nature of sociology. However much Straus may want the sociologist *of* medicine to be based outside particular medical settings it is nevertheless the case that the sociologist, if he is to *be* a sociologist and certainly if he is to conduct any worthwhile research, must not only be inside medical settings, both formal and informal, but intimately involved with practical everyday work in those settings.

Further, the provision of medical care is, of course, the outcome of actions taken by wide ranges of people in a whole complex of formal medical and informal settings. An understanding of such provision can only be gained, therefore, from a consideration of the relationship between action in one situation and action in another. It is not just that we need to analyse interrelationships between action in different situations in order to "get an overall view" or because we think that the various situations all form part of a "medical system". We need to study relationships between various groups and situations in order to understand social action in *any* situation. In short, the understanding of action in a particular illness situation is dependent upon that situation being placed in its social context. For the position of any group within a complex of groups may be said to determine the social conditions of action of the group concerned.

In order to elaborate on this point we can take the everyday medical question of referral. For, the act of referral is an explicit recognition that the provision of medical care involves the interrelationship of activities in many settings. It is, therefore, of particular interest to the sociologist.

Referral

The sociologist is interested in referral behaviour since it, to an extent, reveals more clearly than formal administrative or organizational charts the nature of social relations between various categories of medical and non-medical personnel in formal medical and other situations. In respect of any particular act of referral several common-sense questions can be asked, such as why was X referred from A to B? Who referred X? Why was X referred from A to B at this time? Some of the material from a study of people referred to an out-patient department with alcohol-related problems is cited for purposes of example.[10]

One aspect of this study entailed the analysis of case notes and referral letters. The aim was to discover the range of sources of referral and, if possible, some indication of the criteria employed by those who made referrals. In addition, there was an opportunity to look at the response made by the hospital to particular categories of referral agent. Chapter II concentrated upon the whole series of decisions and considerations affecting the process of initial contact with professional medical agencies. This short section deals with two separate but intimately related points, namely; the criteria for and handling of referals from one medical agency to another, and the criteria and handling of referral from a non-medical agency to a medical one. In short, aspects of G.P.'s and probation officer's referral to an out-patient department are considered.

Referral from medical sources

Butterfield and Wadsworth in their study of Guy's Hospital out-patient referrals,[11] noted that in 27 per cent of referral letters which they analysed no diagnosis was mentioned. The letter merely requested the specialist to "please see and advise". "It was assumed," they said, "that since no diagnosis was mentioned the G.P. did not wish to commit himself to an explanation of the patient's complaint." Clearly, the willingness with which G.P.'s commit themselves to a diagnosis, or an explanation of the patient's complaint, was one of the areas of interest in the study of referral behaviour. A sample of G.P.'s referral letters and accompanying casenotes were inspected. The alcohol-related problems of those referred fell into two clear categories. First, there were people defined unequivocally as "alcoholic" or as having "alcoholism".

"I would be grateful if you would help this lady who is an alcoholic".
"This man is an alcoholic".
"Thank you for seeing Mrs X., she is an alcoholic".

A second category of letters referred to drink in a way which suggested that the G.P. thought a problem might be developing, or that a current problem might worsen. Phrases such as "heavy drinking", "started to drink heavily", and "has started drinking", are typical of the signposting of a *potential* alcoholism diagnosis. There were also some letters in which mention of drink was made *in passing* in conjunction with other specific diagnoses or problems;

". . . depression, fits of temper and drinking".
". . . tends to be violent and has started to drink".

Only one G.P. explicitly acknowledged some difficulty over the definition of alcoholism when he wrote;

"Thank you for seeing this patient for me. He is indeed a problem. I suppose if you define an alcoholic as a man who cannot stop drinking, then Mr X is certainly an alcoholic . . ."

The apparent unwillingness to call Mr X. an alcoholic in spite of the fact that "he drinks ¾–1 bottle of whiskey a day . . .

he also suffers from gout . . ." and that alcohol was ". . . gradually changing his personality . . ." so that he was ". . . becoming agressive and belligerent to his daughters . . ." appeared to be due to the fact that ". . . fortunately his alcoholism has not intruded into his ability in his responsible job. . . ." As Pattison has pointed out[12] many doctors seem reluctant to define as alcoholic a person who is working and retaining his social and, particularly, economic standards; while Blane and co-workers have suggested[13] that alcoholics not conforming to the popular skid-row stereotype may be missed diagnostically. Only one G.P. referred a patient with a drink-related-problem, while at the same time stating categorically that "he is not an alcoholic". The reason why this man was not considered to be an alcoholic was that "he does not drink on Mondays or Tuesdays"!

Finally, in addition to these two categories of letters, there were several letters in which no mention was made of alcoholism or any drink-related problem. However, mention was made in either the case notes or in the reply from the hospital to the G.P. Reasons for these referrals were many and varied, ranging from; ". . . increasingly anxious regarding his loss of libido . . .", via ". . . severe depression" to " . . . very mixed-up, and has made a half-hearted attempt at suicide . . .".

It is not surprising that there should be such a range of drink-related problems referred by G.P.'s to an out-patient department. One of the sociologist's interests in such material, however, is to see how these referrals were handled. That is, for example, to see from the case notes and replies to the G.P.'s how formal diagnoses were arrived at. For as well as presenting diagnoses or sign-posting potential diagnoses some G.P.'s made statements as to the cause and consequences of particular drink-related problems, statements about the patient's motivation to stop drinking or to co-operate with different types of treatment, and statements indicating their expectations of what the out-patient department could do for the particular case under discussion.

However, the presentation of this material was not a uniform feature of all G.P.'s letters. Rather it tended to be specifically presented in relation to those patients whose problem had been defined as "heavy drinking", "excess drinking", "drinking to excess" and so on; rather than those who were defined unequivocably as alcoholic.

These statements as to cause and consequence, motivation, and expectations as to treatment, appeared to be presented by the G.P. as background, filling-out material in order to make the presented picture of the patient as full as possible. In order, that is, for the practitioner in the hospital to confirm or reject what can be conceptualized as the G.P.'s "offer" of an alcoholism diagnosis. The "offered" diagnosis could, thus, be either taken up by the hospital practitioner, ignored, or specifically rejected.

Since, by and large, it is conventional for hospital staff to enter into correspondence with the general practitioners from whom patients are referred, it was possible to inspect *pairs* of letters, where they existed, in order to discover the extent of coincidence between diagnoses or other drink references. From an inspection of several available pairs of letters, it was clear that there was a broad measure of agreement between the placing of patient in broad alcohol-related categories. For instance, all those patients who the G.P. had referred to unequivocably as alcoholic, or as having alcoholism, were similarly referred to by the hospital practitioner in his reply. However, in the category of heavy drinkers, excess drinkers, etc., in relation to which other information about cause, consequence and motivation had been provided by the G.P., the "offered" diagnosis was either taken up by the hospital and transformed into a firm alcoholism diagnosis, or not taken up and no further mention of it was made in either the case notes or in the hospital's reply to the referring G.P.

It is clear, therefore, that any description of the referral of patients from one medical situation to another must be informed by a consideration of what the act of referral means to the people involved and what the implications of the referral are, for example, in terms of the creation of particular diagnoses.

There were very few open disagreements between the referring G.P. and the responding hospital practitioner over diagnoses. However the measure of agreement was rather more apparent than real. This was hinted at by the fact that in several of the cases drink was not mentioned in either the G.P.'s letter or in the reply from the hospital. The designation of these cases as coming within the overall category of patients with drink-related problems came after a close reading of the case notes. From these it soon became clear that replies to G.P.'s from the hospital seemed, in some instances, designed merely to confirm the G.P.'s initial diagnosis, rather than to reveal the diagnosis which had informed the out-patient or in-patient care at the hospital. To take the most clear example, Mr P. aged fifty-six was referred to the emergency clinic with a letter from his G.P. addressed to "Consultant Psychiatrist, Urgent". It read:

> "Dear Doctor, This patient has been strange for the last three weeks, worse last weekend. He says somebody is following him and went to the door last night, and other odd ideas. Very quiet. Not aggressive. Would you please see and advise".

Mr P. was, in fact, admitted immediately as an in-patient. A letter, subsequently sent from the hospital to the G.P., spoke at length of depression, paranoid ideas, the investigation which had been carried out and the treatment which had been given. The patient was "returned to your care". There was no mention at all of alcoholism, drink, or any drink-related problem. However, the in-patient case notes referred in the initial formulation to ". . . a fifty-six year old alcoholic man of low intelligence" while the "internal instructions to the sister or nurse in charge" described the patient as "an alcoholic" and asked for "evidence of disorientation, memory loss, also of hallucinations and delusions and incipient D.T.'s".

The instruction ended by saying that the patient would "no doubt try to get a drink".

This specific material on out-patient referrals discusses only formal medical records and correspondence. It has nothing to report on the drinker's self-definition or on their notions of what would count as being an alcoholic. However, it is reasonable to assume that referral with some drink-related problem to a specialist out-patient clinic would not have been an insignificant episode for the drinker even if the "offered" alcoholism diagnoses was eventually rejected.[14] For, the process of becoming an alcoholic is, in part, the process of the development of diagnosis of "alcoholism" in the course of everyday interchanges between medical and non-medical personnel in formal and informal medical settings.

Those letters in which the specialist did not reveal the diagnosis which informed the hospital care which was given to the patient, but merely returned the G.P.'s description of the patient's problem, were in a sense *private* diagnoses of alcoholism. The question of the implications of such private diagnoses, for subsequent intra-professional communication and for the relationship between the patient and his G.P., is one which can only be raised here. But where the specialist upgraded either an offered diagnosis or passing drink-reference into a firm diagnosis of alcoholism, it can be assumed that the G.P. would adopt this diagnosis and present it himself on any subsequent referral. In the very small number of cases where information was available on the re-referral of such patients this would seem to be so. Similarly, since the diagnosis would then be clear, and to an extent "decided upon", the whole host of statements about cause, consequence and motivation would tend to disappear. In short, the process of the construction of the diagnosis of alcoholism, and thus the process of becoming an alcoholic, would have gone a stage further.

Referral from non-medical sources

Just as people are referred to out-patient departments by medical professionals so they are referred by certain well-defined non-medical agencies. Clearly, not all non-medical people have the same access to scarce medical resources. While referrals from probation officers or social workers may be considered legitimate by out-patient staff, people are rarely referred by butchers, bakers or candlestick makers. Suppose several people came to an out-patient clinic with letters saying:

> "This man is an alcoholic, please see and advise. Signed:
> J. Cleaver, (Butcher, 18 High Street)".

In all probability these patients would either be sent away to consult their G.P.'s who would decide whether a referral was necessary, or they would be seen as the emergency clinic, but categorized as self-referrals. In any event, Mr Cleaver, the butcher, would almost certainly not receive the standard letter thanking him for his referrals, he would not be informed of the treatments which were undertaken, or told about the outcome of the cases which he "referred". The patients would certainly not be "returned to your care". In short, Mr Cleaver would be considered a non-person as far as the taken-for-granted everyday referral mechanisms of the hospital were concerned. But while Mr Cleaver may be a non-person, not all non-medical-professional people are so categorized. Social workers and probation officers, for example, are people who, in certain circumstances, act in the same way as medical professionals and such action is considered to be acceptable. Clearly, the sociologist is interested in how such situations are handled.

In the already mentioned study of referral behaviour,[15] several people with alcohol-related problems were referred to the out-patient department by probation officers. Such referrals were of two main types. First, people referred for medical attention and advice;

> "The above-named is on prison after-care to me at this office,
> he has been drinking continuously for the past ten days. . . ."

and second, people referred by the probation officer for a psychiatrist's report in relation to remand requirements at a magistrate's court;

> "... she appeared at ... magistrate's court and pleaded guilty to stealing about £40 from one of her friends ... she was remanded for a probation officer's report and a psychiatrist's report until ...."

In spite of the fact that specific diagnoses and references to the cause and consequences of drink-related problems were sparse, all the probation service referrals were accepted by the out-patient department. Psychiatric reports were forwarded, on time, in respect of remand cases and in the other cases courses of treatment and series of consultations were planned. However, the legitimacy of the referral and the nature of the relationship between the probation officer and the hospital medical staff, as revealed in the correspondence about cases, was clearly informed by the legal status of the case. In the event of a remand-related consultation the correspondence was of that between two equals, courteous but not ingratiating. Both had parts to play *vis-à-vis* the legal process. Both gave full and open accounts of the case to each other.

However, when a probation officer tried to refer someone direct to the hospital *purely for medical help* the situation was rather different. Although such cases were accepted, the notion of "different but equal" experts was not in evidence. In the majority of cases which were referred by probation officers for purely medical reasons no reply was sent to them from the hospital. In some cases a reply was sent but only in order to rebuke the referring officer. For example, in response to a probation officer who sent a man with a very short accompanying letter to the emergency clinic, the psychiatrist wrote;

> "Thank you for referring this patient whom I saw in the emergency clinic on ... June. I understand from the patient

> that his G.P. did not know he had been referred here. However,
> I have sent a full report to him and suggested a course of
> treatment. I think in future it might be better if you get a
> patient's G.P. to refer him/her to . . . hospital who can then
> give us any medical history that we require when seeing the
> patient. Yours sincerely . . ."

The case was, thus, immediately taken out of the probation
officer's sphere of influence. What his working relationship
with the patient was is uncertain since he did not reveal it in
his short referral letter. Perhaps this was where he went
wrong. However, the reply to the probation officer from the
hospital did not mention the diagnosis, or the course of treatment which had been initiated. In fact, the patient had been
given an appointment to see a consultant who specialized in
alcohol-related problems. The patient was described as 'having
". . . some symptoms of depression and anxiety state" which
"may well have exacerbated his drinking problem which is
serious". The effective isolation of the probation officer from the
medical aspects of the case was further strengthened when in
the hospital's letter to the patient's G.P. the referral agent was
not mentioned by name.

> "Dear Doctor, . . . Your patient was referred to us by a
> probation officer at . . . magistrates court and appeared with
> a letter written two weeks ago . . ."

Several referrals, however, demonstrated the technique for
overcoming this intra-professional problem. One such case
was, in purely medical terms, less acute than the case which
elicited the rebuke from the hospital staff.

> "He now has a high degree of social inadequacy which he has
> covered by excessive use of alcohol . . . ambivalent feelings
> towards authority and institutions . . ."

But the probation officer presented it properly. The referral
letter began with a flowery introduction:

> "It is with Mr X's knowledge and consent – indeed at his request that I tried to get him such help – that I am writing to you today . . ."

it proceeded to a full case history, including a probation report from Australia where the patient had lived for several years, detailed the current state of the patient,

> "Comparatively speaking spent only a short time outside prison walls . . . he is a behavioural and social problem . . . has been described as of low intelligence".

and indicated a recent change in the patient's motivation towards treatment and life generally. The letter ended by pointing out that the case was special, and that the probation officer knew that such a referral was unusual. It tentatively requested the possibility of an appointment,

> I wonder if you would be prepared to accept this as a direct referral and consider arranging for him to be seen as an out-patient. Yours sincerely . . ."

The protracted account of one small aspect of one small study of some referrals to one out-patient department does not tell us anything very new about probation officers, psychiatrists, hospitals, alcoholism, or alcoholics. It has been presented rather to indicate how action in any particular situation cannot be understood without taking into account the social organizational context of that situation. Just as the relationship between patient and doctor is "an exchange between two elements of society rather than two individuals",[16] so the relationship between G.P. and hospital practitioner, or probation officer and hospital practitioner, is not between individuals; but individuals in so far as they occupy particular positions in relation to others in particular settings at particular times.

To an extent, it is easy to close off particular situations and think of them *as if* they existed in isolation. But, as was noted in the previous chapter, often the most important features of particular situations are determined by the relationship between action in one situation and action in another. As the material from the referral study has indicated, any description of, for example, the type of patient seen at an out-patient clinic must take into account the everyday rules for handling referrals operated by the staff of that clinic, the criteria of definition and diagnoses used by particular categories of referral agent, and their ideas about appropriate places to refer particular categgories of people with whom they come into contact. Such considerations are not only a matter of interest for the sociologist, but obviously have implications for any study of the causation of disorders based upon treaty populations or cases in particular settings; and for those who have administrative or planning interests or responsibilities.

The sociologist in *illness situations*

> . . . participant observation, field observation, qualitative observation, direct observation, or field research . . . refer to the circumstances of being in or around an ongoing social setting for the purpose of making a qualitative analysis of that setting. This may not be the person's sole purpose for being present, but it is at least an important one. *Lofland.*[17]

At the end of the previous chapter, in a short note on questionnaire inquiry, it was claimed that if the sociologist is to understand social interaction in particular medical settings he must rely on something other than replies to questions asked of individuals outside those settings. In short, since social interaction is situationally defined he must participate in some way in those situations. But by having access in some way to a particular medical setting the sociologist is, of course, raising as well as solving methodological problems. If he stands apart from illness situations and conducts his inquiry through questionnaires he loses the opportunity to become immersed in the medical context and to become familiar with the everyday rules which structure action in that context and with the problems and difficulties which characterize medical care. On the other hand, if he becomes too immersed in the medical context he may lose his distinctive perspective and, by being a participant, come to identify with a particular ideology, set of values or assumptions, which it should be his task to tease out, analyse, and indicate the implications of. Clearly, this is the field worker's basic dilemma and is the subject, naturally, of a continuing debate in all the social sciences.[18] The two main methods of participant inquiry by the sociologists are either by being an unknown observer or a known observer. There are strengths and weakness in each approach.[19]

Unknown observers

As a research strategy, the observer may join a group, take a job or in some other way enter a setting as a participant for the purpose of observing it. Such a strategy is limited, of course, to those opportunities which are already open to the sociologist *as a person*. In the medical sphere such an approach would not enable the sociologist to study social relations in an operating theatre but could quite easily allow him to study social relations in a G.P.'s waiting room or a hospital out-patient department. But it may be that involvement in some capacity in a medical situation precedes the decision to attempt an analysis of that situation. This was the case with Roth's study of a tuberculosis hospital[20] which developed out of the situation of Roth's patient status. But whether the involvement comes prior to the decision to observe or vice versa the observer *as an observer* remains unknown to all other members of the setting.

Such an approach has advantages and disadvantages. Observing people without telling them may be considered an immoral activity in itself, and certainly some sociologists feel that people should never be observed without their knowledge. Others feel that the practice is acceptable if the research report is presented in such a way as to make impossible the identification of particular individuals or particular settings.[21] Such anonymity is likely to be much more easy to maintain when the study is done in a common medical setting, such as a general practice, rather than an uncommon one, such as a heart transplant unit. The chances of the latter setting remaining unidentifiable are obviously slender.

The major research restriction of being an unknown observer is that the observer will, by definition, be restricted to occupying one particular social position in the setting. To use the role of the patient in a hospital as a base for unknown observation means that the sociologist is not free to wander about the ward, or to gain access to meetings, research, records, conversations, or settings, which would not in the normal course of events be available to a patient in that ward. The unknown observer is clearly less free than the known observer to question others in the situation about their ideas and actions, and less free also to withdraw in order to think or write.

On the other hand, the unknown observer has one vital advantage in his quest to gain an understanding of the everyday practices of a particular situation. He is acted towards as an everyday participant and, thus, can observe and gain a knowledge of the setting from a real, rather than an artificial, position. From such a position he will be likely to gain an intimate understanding of the perspective of at least some participants in the situation by being seen to be, and being acted towards as, a full participant. Finally, it may be that being an unknown observer is the only way in which a setting can be observed. Thus, the choice may be between occupying a particular position in the setting or not observing the setting at all.

The known observer

The most obvious advantage of being a *known* observer in any situation is freedom to play the role of observer. That is, the freedom to ask questions which would not normally be asked, to move about and observe in a range of setting which no other person occupying any *particular* position would be able to do because of notions about appropriate behaviour for particular people. The difficulty of being a participant as well as being an observer is overcome and the known observer can represent himself as such. This does not mean that he will be accepted or spoken to or liked, but at least his position will be clear, open and not disguised.

There are, of course, difficulties with being a known observer. The first concerns the problem of initial access, since by definition this is likely to be at the request of or with the permission of higher participants. The sociologist would not be able to do work in St. Thomas's by asking the permission of only the patients, or in Pentonville by asking only the prisoners, or at Eton only the pupils, or at Ford's only the workers on the shop floor. Gaining entry, as a known observer, *from the top* has clear disadvantages since particular categories of participants are quite reasonably going to see the observer as working *for* the higher participants. The higher participants may actually define the situation in this way themselves and it is essential for the sociologist in a medical setting to make it clear that he is not working *for* anyone. His task is to gain an understanding of social action in particular situations. Certainly, the report of any piece of social investigation may undermine cherished beliefs or question long established truths accepted by various categories of participants. But, as was stressed in Chapter I, it is not the sociologist's aim *as a sociologist* to achieve this, any more than it is his aim to comfort, or approve, or acclaim, particular positions, practices or procedures.

Several difficulties for the known observer are set out and discussed in Lofland's introduction to "Analysing Social Settings".[22] He lists these as *factions*, ". . . in entering as a known observer, there arises the question of the observer's stance relative to local disputes and alliances", *loyalty* ". . . in our cultural tradition, the observer smacks of the 'spy' and the possible 'sell out'. His loyalties are not evidently to the setting or to any of its factions", *marginality* "there is . . . a subtle separation between the observer and the members that can be painful and poignant 'you are here or you know, but yet you are not really one of us'. . . . If it is any consolation, it is out of this circumstance of being the marginal man – the simultaneous insider-outsider – that creative insight is best generated", and *personal involvement* "to what degree should the would-be neutral observer respond to the pain and difficulty he must inevitably observe if he is close?". In connection with this see, for example, Herbert Gans' account of his temptation to stop the research resulting in "The Urban Villagers" and instead fight a local "urban renewal".

One of the most revealing accounts of the introduction of an academic social scientist into a specialist medical setting is Renée Fox's "Experiment Perilous: physicians and patients facing the unknown". In this book she describes her study of an all-male fifteen-bed, metabolic research ward in a New England teaching hospital. Because procedures like adrenalectomy, haemeodialysis and renal transplant were radical and still largely untried they were attempted only on patients who were acutely, seriously, and often terminally, ill; patients who, as one doctor put it "could well be dead the next day".[23] Fox says of "Experiment Perilous" that it was

> . . . a study of the physicians of the metabolic group and the patients of Ward F-Second. It focuses particularly on various problems these physicians and patients encountered in this setting, some of the strains they experienced as a consequence, their ways of trying to cope with those problems and stresses and some of the observed consequences of the ways of coming to terms they evolved.

In such a setting the problems of being "an observer" were particularly acute. The situation was highly charged, stressful, specialized, and cut off from the outside world. Her presence as an observer was known from the outset. She was a sociologist and, as such, had no medical technique, knowledge or skill to offer and no position as "fellow patient" to build upon. In the following extended quotation Renée Fox describes some of her decisions about being a known observer and her acceptance on Ward F-Second.

> The first adrenalectomies had been performed, the first psychiatric interviews had been conducted, when I was asked to join this collaborative enterprise. What the function of the sociologist was to be, however, had not really been ascertained, for this was the first time that these two groups of physicians had ever had the occasion to work with an academic social scientist . . .
>
> We agreed that F-Second (the ward on which the metabolic group's most important research pateints were housed) should be my site of operations. But it was to me to decide how I would present myself to the community; and to plan out my daily round. Recalling the openness of the sick world from my own patient days (as a polio case) – its candour and its remarkable grape-vine – I felt it would be wiser to appear on the ward as the sociologist I actually was than to assume a form of camouflage. "Passing" as a volunteer, a ward maid, a clerk – all might have their advantages, perhaps. But it seemed to me that given the known tendencies of the patient world (along with my own lack of talent for subterfuge), the probability of being found out ran very high. Rather than risk the consequences of such a disclosure, then, I was willing to pay the penalties of non-concealment. (The losses of such a frank approach, I imagined, might consist in increased restraint on the part of the patients, and in their reluctance to grant me access to certain ward intimacies.)
>
> However, it was not purely as a classroom sociologist that I planned to make an appearance. To certify my presence in the eyes of the patients and the medical team (I determined) I would adopt a white coat. I would be introduced to F-Second Ward by those medical team members who had the closest first-hand relationship to it – the nurses. And I would make myself visibly useful by undertaking those ward tasks that did not interfere with my observations. By participating in the life of the ward in this way, I felt, I would gain more rapid and complete acceptance into the ward community. My decision to be a relatively active observer was also influenced by my inner need to do something more than just watch, listen, and take notes in the presence of such urgent human situations as one finds in

a hospital ward. Thus, the role which I chose to play was one which would not only involve attributes of a thesis-writing graduate student making sociological observations but also those of an ancillary member of a medical team, helping the doctors and nurses with some of the work which had to be done.

Though my ex-patient status was an important and relevant fact, I did not intend to include it in my self-presentation. To be sure, it was the part of my inner equipment – both prejudicial and enlightening. However, because I hoped to understand the ward as a living totality – from the point of view of its physicians as well as patients – I did not wish to be overly identified with either. Discretion about my former illness, I felt, would be a precaution against too closely aligning myself with the patients.

But I had not accounted for Leo Angelico. Sensitized to walking impediments by his own wheel-chair plight, Leo took instant note of my subtle limp. In the outspoken way of a veteran patient, he asked me if I had been a "polio"; and with the same frankness I answered affirmatively. By the day's end the "news" of my patienthood had travelled the length of the ward. From that time on, I was known as Miss Fox: Ward Sociologist and ex-patient. In the months that followed, whenever my ability to "really understand" the ward was questioned the answer of the old-timers was always the same: "But Miss Fox *does* understand – because she was a patient herself!" In this respect, then, it was my own experience of illness and hospitalization (more than any other single fact) which speeded my acceptance by the men of Ward F-Second and validated my study in their eyes.

What this demonstrates is a basic property not only of participant observation but of social interaction in general. The roles that a person assumes – the ways they are defined, structured, and played out – are never completely self-determined. Rather, they emerge as a joint product of the dynamic relationships between an individual and other persons with whom he or she is interacting.

This, I think, shows the essential difference between the kind of research which is possible based upon participant observation and that which would be possible – at one remove – by means of questionnaires. Each approach has strengths and weaknesses. The vital point is to be clear about the nature of the research question which is being asked and to design any particular study to best tackle that question. By and large any question about *social* relations as opposed to individual opinions or characteristics will need an observer/interviewer rather than a questionnaire approach.

Sociology and medicine: a concluding note

> I think that sociological concepts and methods do have merit as approaches to clinical problems in medicine. . . . But I have sometimes found the doctors who act with proper precaution when a medical definition is at issue throw it to the wind when they come to consider social categorization. *Jefferys.*[24]

This short book has not attempted to discuss every medical topic which is of interest to the sociologist, or every action of the sociologist which might be of interest to the medical practitioner. The aim has been to indicate something of the sociologist's approach to the question of health, illness and medical care, in order that others may have a realistic idea of what it is that the sociologist is up to when he is "being a sociologist", and thus, what it is and is not reasonable to expect him to do or to say *as* a sociologist in relation to medicine.

Briefly, the book has attempted to demonstrate that the sociologist is concerned to understand everyday life. The medical sociologist is engaged in the attempt to describe social action in illness-related situations in order that all those concerned may have a closer acquaintance with the meaning and implications of any illness episode for the symptomatic person, significant lay and professional others, and the wider society. The sociologist seeks to illuminate and explain the various lay and professional perspectives through which these episodes are viewed. Such perspectives will vary from situation to situation and over time in accordance with people's values, beliefs and experience of life, and these variations will have implications for the provision and outcome of medical care.

Suggestions for further reading:

Fox, R. C. *Experiment Perilous: physicians and patients facing the unknown.* Free Press, Glencoe, Illinois, 1959.

Jefferys, M. Sociology and Medicine: separation or symbiosis? *Lancet*, i, iiii, 1969.

Kitsuse, J. and Cicourel, A. V. A note on the uses of official statistics *Social Problems*, 12, 131, 1963.

Lofland, J. *Analysing Social Settings.* Prentice-Hall, Englewood Cliffs, New Jersey, 1971.

Sigerist, H. E. *A History of Medicine.* Oxford University Press, London, 1951.

Straus, R. The Nature and Status of Medical Sociology. *Amer. Sociol. Rev.*, 22, 200, 1957.

REFERENCES

Introduction

(1) *The Genuine Works of Hippocrates*. Williams & Wilkins, Baltimore, 1939.
(2) General Medical Council. *Recommendations as to Basic Medical Education*. London, 1967.
(3) *Royal Commission on Medical Education Report*. H.M.S.O., London 1968.
(4) Reader, G. G. Contributions to Sociology of Medicine. In Freeman, H. E. *et al.*, *Handbook of Medical Sociology*. Prentice-Hall Inc., Englewood Cliffs, N.J., 1963.
(5) For example: Mechanic, D. *Medical Sociology: a selective view*. New York Free Press, 1968 and Coe, R. M. *Sociology of Medicine*. McGraw-Hill, New York, 1970.
(6) For example: Becker, H. S. *et al. Boys in White: student culture in medical school*. Chicago Univ. Press, Chicago, 1961 and Coser, R. L. *Life in the Ward*. Michigan State Univ. Press, Michigan, 1962.
(7) For example: Inkeles, A. *What is Sociology?* Prentice-Hall Inc. Englewood Cliffs, N.J., 1964 and Bottomore, T. B. *Sociology*. George Allen & Unwin, London, 1962.

Chapter I.   The Sociologist's Viewpoint

(1) Virchow, R. *Scientific Methods and Therapeutic Standpoints*. 1849.
(2) Parsons, T. *The Structure of Social Action*. McGraw-Hill, New York, 1937.
(3) Durkheim, E. *The Rules of Sociological Method*. (First published 1848). Free Press, New York, 1964.
(4) Weber, M. Economy and Society. (Wirtschaft und Gesellschaft, published posthumously in 1921). The first part is available in English translated by A. M. Henderson and Talcott Parsons as Max Weber: *The Theory of Social and Economic Organization*. New York, 1947.
(5) Rex, J. *Key Problems of Sociological Theory*. Routledge and Kegan Paul, London, 1961.
(6) Stacey, M. *et al. Hospitals, Children and their Families*. Routledge & Kegan Paul, London, 1970.
(7) H.M.S.O. *The Welfare of Children in Hospital*. London, 1959.
(8) MacCarthy, D. *Brit. Med. J.*, 1, 1008, 1964.
(9) Meadow, S. R. *Brit. Med. J.*, 1, 813, 1964.
(10) Riley, D. *et al. Brit. Med. J.*, 2, 990, 1965.

(11) Durkheim, E. *The Rules of Sociological Method* op. cit. 1964.
(12) Lynd, R. *Knowledge for What?* Princeton University Press, Princeton, 1939.
(13) Weber, M. op. cit. 1947.

Chapter II. Becoming Ill: a Bio-social Process

(1) Kosa, J. *et al. The Place of Morbid Episodes in the Social Interaction Pattern.* Paper read to the 6th Congress of the International Sociological Association, Evian, France, 1966.
(2) Mechanic, D. The Concept of Illness Behaviour. *J. Chron. Dis.,* 15, 189, 1961.
(3) Douglas, J. *Understanding Everyday Life.* Routledge & Kegan Paul, London, 1971.
(4) For an excellent review see Mandelbaum, D. G. Alcohol and Culture. *Current Anthropology,* 6, 3, 281–293, 1965.
(5) Mulford, H. A. Alcoholism a Concern (and Creation) of Every Community. *Selected Papers,* 18th Annual Meeting, N.A.A.A.P., Chicago, 3–15, 1967.
(6) Wing, J. K. International Comparisons in the Study of Functional Psychoses. *Brit. Med. Bull.,* 27, 1, 77–81, 1971.
(7) For a discussion of this point in relation to alcoholism see Robinson, D. The Alcohologist's Addiction: some implications of having lost control over the disease concept of alcoholism. *Quart. J. Stud. Alc.,* 33, 4, 1028, 1972.
(8) Jellinek, E. M. *The Disease Concept of Alcoholism.* New Haven, Hillhouse Press, 1960.
(9) Ireland, Father John. The Catholic Church and the Saloon. *North American Review,* CLIX, 502, 1894.
(10) Keller, M. The Definition of Alcoholism. *Quart. J. Stud. Alc.,* 21, 125–134, 1960.
(11) Edwards, G. The Status of Alcoholism as a Disease, in Phillipson, R. V. (Ed.), *Modern Trends in Drug Dependence and Alcoholism.* Butterworths, London, 1970.
(12) Seeley, J. The Making and Taking of Problems. *Soc. Problems,* XIV, 1966.
(13) Coe, R. M. *Sociology of Medicine.* McGraw-Hill Book Co., New York, 1970.
(14) Morris, J. N. *Uses of Epidemiology.* 2nd Ed. E. & S. Livingstone, Edinburgh and London, 1964. Paul, J. R. *Clinical Epidemiology.* Univ. of Chicago Press, Chicago, 1958.
(15) Commission on Chronic Illness. *Chronic Illness in a Large City.* Harvard University Press, Cambridge, 1957.
(16) Pearce, I. H. and Crocker, L. H. *The Peckham Experiment.* Allen & Unwin, London, 1954.

(17) Hinkle, L. E. *et al*. An examination of the relation between symptoms, disability and serious illness in two homogeneous groups of men and women. *Am. J. Public Health, 50, 1327*, 1960.

(18) Suchman, E. A. The addictive diseases as socio-environmental health problems. In Freeman, H. E. *et al*. (Eds.), *Handbook of Medical Sociology*, Prentice-Hall Inc. Englewood Cliffs, New Jersey, 1963.

(19) Robinson, D. *The Process of Becoming Ill*. Routledge & Kegan Paul, London, 1971.

(20) Selznick, P. *Leadership in Administration*. Harper & Row, London, 1957.

(21) Robinson, D. op. cit. 1971.

(22) Gibson, Q. *The Logic of Social Enquiry*. Routledge & Kegan Paul, London, 1960.

(23) Zola, I. K. Illness behaviour of the working class: implications and recommendations. In Shostak, A. B. and Gomberg, W. (Eds.), *Blue Collar World*. Prentice-Hall Inc. Englewood Cliffs, N.J., 1964.

(24) Howe, G. M. (compiler). *National Atlas of Disease Mortality*. Nelson, London, 1968.

(25) Dubos, R. *Mirage of Health*. Anchor, Garden City, New York, 1961.

Chapter III. The Patient: a Social Position

(1) Balint, M. *The Doctor, his Patient and the Illness*. Tavistock Publications, London, 1964.

(2) Mechanic, D. The Concept of Illness Behaviour. *J. Chron. Dis., 15, 189*, 1961.

(3) For a very clear review of a lot of the literature see Kasl, S. V. and Cobb, S. Health behaviour, illness behaviour and sick role behaviour. *Arch. Environmental Health, 12, 246*, 1966.

(4) See for example. Gordon, G. *Role Theory and Illness*. College & Univ. Press, New Haven, Conn., 1966 and Twaddle, A. C., Health Decisions and sick role variations: an exploration. *J. Health and Social Behaviour, 10, 105*, 1969.

(5) Parsons, T. *The Social System*. Free Press, Chicago, 1951.

(6) Sigerist, H. E. The Special Position of the Sick. First written in 1929 and now republished in Roemer, M. I. *Sigerist on the Sociology of Medicine*. M.D. Publications, New York, 1960.

(7) Parsons, T. op. cit. 1951.

(8) Gordon, R. op. cit., 1966. Twaddle, A. C. op. cit. 1969.

(9) Parsons, T. op. cit. 1951.

(10) Glueck, B. C. Changing concepts in forensic psychiatry. *The Journal of Criminal Law, Criminology and Police Science*, XLV, 123, 1954–55.

(11) Cited in Margolis, P. *Psychotherapy and Morality: a study of two concepts*. Random House Inc., New York, 1966.

(12)   Roche, P. *The Criminal Mind*. Farrar, Straws and Cudahy, New York, 1958.

(13)   Wootton, B. *Social Science and Social Pathology*. George Allen & Unwin, London, 1959.

(14)   Zacune, J. and Hensman, C. (compilers). *Drugs, Alcohol and Tobacco in Britain*. Heinemann Medical Books, London, 1971.

(15)   Parsons, T. op. cit. 1951.

(16)   Robinson, D. op. cit. 1971.

(17)   Gordon, G. op. cit. 1951.

(18)   Di Cicco, L. and Apple, D. Health needs and symptoms of older adults. In Apple, D. (Ed.), *Sociological Studies of Health and Sickness*. McGraw-Hill, New York, 1960.

(19)   Schneider, D. The Social Dynamics of Physical Disability in Army Basic Training. *Psychiatry, 10, 323,* 1947.

(20)   Koos, E. *The Health of Regionville – what the people thought and did about it*. Columbia Univ. Press, New Jersey, 1954.

(21)   Zborowski, M. Cultural Components in Responses to Pain. *Journal of Social Issues, 8, 16,* 1952.

(22)   Knutson, A. *The Individual, Society and Health Behaviour*. Russell Sage Foundation, New York, 1965.

(23)   Parsons, T. op. cit. 1951.

Chapter IV.   Patient and Doctor: a Social Relationship

(1)   Bastide, R. *The Sociology of Mental Disorder*. (Trans. McNeil, J.) Routledge & Kegan Paul, London, 1972.

(2)   Weber, M. Economy and Society. (Wirtschaft und Gesellschaft). First part (trans.) Henderson, A. M. and Parsons, T. as *The Theory of Social and Economic Organisation*. New York, 1947.

(3)   Ibid.

(4)   Fox, R. C. *Experiment Perilous*. Free Press, Glencoe, Illnois, 1959.

(5)   Koos, E. *The Health of Regionville: what the people thought and did about it*. Columbia Univ. Press, New York, 1954.

(6)   Freidson, E. Client Control and Medical Practice. *Amer. J. Siociol.,* 65, 374, 1960.

(7)   Clyne, M. G. *Night Calls: a study in general practice*. Tavistock Publications, London, 1961.

(8)   Mechanic, D. *Medical Sociology*. Free Press, New York, 1968.

(9)   Freidson, E. *Profession of Medicine: a study of the sociology of applied knowledge*. Dodd Mead, New York, 1972.

(10)   Ibid.

(11)   Szasz, T. and Hollander, M. H. A Contribution to the Philosophy of Medicine. *A.M.A. Archives of Internal Medicine, XCVII, 585,* 1956.

(12)   Ibid.

(13)   Freidson, op. cit. 1972.

(14) Duff, S. and Hollingshead, A. B. *Sickness and Society*. Harper & Row, New York, 1968.

(15) Friedson, E. op. cit. 1972.

(16) Balint, M. *The Doctor, his Patient and the Illness*. Tavistock Publications, London, 1964.

(17) Roth, J. A. *Timetables: Structuring the Passage of Time in Hospital and Other Careers*. Dobbs-Merrill & Co., Indianapolis, 1963.

(18) Parsons, T. *The Social System*. Free Press, Chicago, 1951.

(19) Fox, R. C. op. cit. 1959.

(20) Skipper, J. K. (Jnr.). Communication on the Hospital Patient. In Skipper, J. K. (Jnr.) and Leonard, R. C. (Eds.), *Social Interaction and Patient Care*. Lippincott, Philadelphia, 1965.

(21) Cushing, H. *The Life of Sir William Osler*. Cited in Freidson, E., op. cit. 1972.

(22) Scheff, T. Decision Rules, Types of Error and the Consequences in Medical Diagnosis. *Behavioural Science, 8, 97*, 1963.

(23) Parsons, T. op. cit. 1951.

(24) Robinson, D. *The Process of Becoming Ill*. Routledge & Kegan Paul, London, 1971.

(25) Scheff, T. op. cit. 1963.

(26) Garland, L. H. Studies in the Accuracy of Diagnostic Procedures. *Amer. J. Roentgenol., 82, 25*, 1959.

(27) Cochrane, A. L. *et al.*, Observers' Errors in taking Medical Histories. *Lancet, CCLX, 1007*, 1951.

(28) Meador, C. K. The Art and Science of Non-Disease. *New England J. of Med., CCLXXII, 92*, 1965.

(29) Goffman, E. *Stigma: notes on the management of spoiled identity*. Spectrum Books, Englewood Cliffs, New Jersey, 1963.

(30) Lerner, M. and Anderson, O. *Health Progress in the United States: 1900–1960*. Univ. Chicago Press, Chicago, 1963.

(31) Koos, E. op. cit. 1954.

(32) Mechanic, D. op. cit. 1968.

(33) Mechanic, D. op. cit. 1968.

(34) Bastide, R. op. cit. 1972.

Chapter V. Medicine: a Particular Profession

(1) Koos, E. *The Health of Regionville: what the people thought and did about it*. Columbia Univ. Press, New York, 1954.

(2) Freidson, E. *Profession of Medicine: A study of the sociology of applied knowledge*. Dodd, Mead & Co., New York, 1972.

(3) Becker, H. S. The Nature of a Profession. In National Society for the Study of Education. *Education for the Professions*. Chicago, 1962.

(4) Flerner, A. Is Social Work a Profession? *School and Society I*, 1915.

(5) Goode, W. J. The Librarian: From occupation to profession. *The Library Quarterly*. XXI, 1961.

(6) General Register Office. *Classification of Occupations*. H.M.S.O., London, 1970.

(7) See discussion in Bottomore, T. *Classes in Modern Society*. George Allen and Unwin, London, 1966.

(8) Caplow, T. *The Sociology of Work*. McGraw-Hill, New York, 1954.

(9) Cogan, M. I. Toward Definition of Professions. *Harvard Educational Review, XXIII, 33,* 1953.

(10) Goode, W. J. Encroachment, Charlatanism, and the Emerging Profession: Psychology, Medicine and Sociology. *American Sociological Review, XXV, 902,* 1960.

(11) Denzin, N. R. and Mettlin, C. J. Incomplete Professionalisation: the case of pharmacy. *Social Forces, XVLI, 375,* 1968.

(12) Freidson, E. op. cit. 1972.

(13) Ibid.

(14) See, for example, Sigerist, H. E. *A History of Medicine*. Oxford University Press, 1951, and Wilson, L. *The Academic Man: a study in the sociology of a profession*. Oxford University Press, 1942.

(15) Freidson, E. op. cit. 1972.

(16) Ibid.

(17) Burton, R. *Anatomy of Melancholy* (1961). 12th Ed. London, 1821.

(18) Hyde, D. R. *et al*. The American Medical Association: power, purpose and policies in organised medicine. *Yale Law Journal, LXIII, 938,* 1954.

(19) Stevens, R. *Medical Practice in Modern England*. Yale Univ. Press, New Haven, 1966.

(20) Field, M. G. *Soviet Socialised Medicine: an introduction*. Free Press, New York, 1967.

(21) Feldstein, P. J. Research on the demand for Health Services. *Milbank Memorial Fund Quarterly, XLIV, 2, 138,* 1966.

(22) Freidson, E. op. cit. 1972.

(23) Merton, R. *et al. The Student Physician*. Harvard University Press, Cambridge, 1957.

(24) Becker, H. S. *et al. Boys in White: student culture in a medical school*. Univ. Chicago Press, Chicago, 1961.

(25) Phillips, B. S. Expected Value Deprivation and Occupational Preference. *Sociometry, XXVII, 151,* 1964.

(26) Cahalan, D. Career Interests and Expectations of U.S. Medical Students. *J. Med. Educ., XXXII, 558,* 1957.

(27) Schumacher, C. F. Interest and Personality Factors as Related to Choice of Medical Career. *J. Med. Educ., XXXVIII, 932,* 1963.

(28) Bloom, S. N. The Sociology of Medical Education: some comments

on the state of a field. *Milbank Memorial Fund Quarterly, XLIII, 143,* 1965.

(29) Becker, H. S. *et al.* op. cit. 1961.

(30) Ibid.

(31) Ibid.

(32) Sharaf, M. R. and Levinson, D. J. The Quest for Omnipotence in Medical Training. *Psychiatry, XXVII, 141,* 1964.

(33) Caplow, T. op. cit. 1954.

(34) Jackson, D. M. and Short, D. S. The Distinctive Christian Ethics in Medical Practice. In Edmunds, V. and Scorer, C. G. (Eds.), *Medical Ethics: A christian approach.* Tyndale Press, London, 1966.

(35) Anderson, J. A. D. *et al. Brit. Med. J., 1, 108,* 1972.

(36) Brock, Lord. *Brit. Med. J., 1, 440,* 1972.

(37) Caplow, T. op. cit. 1954.

(38) Jackson, D. M. *Professional Ethics: who makes the rules?* C.M.F. Publications, London, 1972.

(39) Briggs, A. E. Social Distance between Lawyers and Doctors. *Sociology and Social Research, 13,* 1948.

(40) Davis, F. (Ed.) *The Nursing Profession.* John Wiley and Sons, New York, 1966. Abel-Smith, B. *A History of the Nursing Profession.* Heinemann, London, 1960.

(41) See Roberts, M. *American Nursing: History and interpretation.* MacMillan, New York, 1954.

(42) Habenstein, R. W. and Christ, E. A. *Professionalizer, Traditionalizer, Utilizer: an interpretative study of the work of the general duty nurse in non-metropolitan Central Missouri general hospitals.* Univ. Missouri Press, Columbia, Missouri, 1955.

(43) Freidson, E. op. cit. 1972.

(44) This section relies heavily upon Zola, I. K. Medicine as an Institution of Social Control. *Soc. Rev. No. 4,* 1972.

(45) Kahn, J. H. Beyond the Determinary Principle. *Applied Social Studies, 1, 73,* 1969.

(46) Freidson, E. op. cit. 1972.

(47) Zola, I. K. op. cit. 1972.

(48) Ibid.

(49) Freidson, E. op. cit. 1972.

(50) Ibid.

Chapter VI. The Hospital: a Complex Organization

(1) Etzioni, A. *Modern Organisations.* Prentice-Hall, Englewood Cliffs, New Jersey, 1964.

(2) See Etzioni, Ibid. For an account of such studies.

(3) Gulick, L. and Urwick, L. (Eds.) *Papers on the Science of Administration.* Columbia Univ., New York, 1937.

(4) Etzioni, A. op. cit. 1964.

(5) Smith, G. *Social Work and the Sociology of Organisations*. Routledge & Kegan Paul, London, 1970.

(6) Blau, P. M. *The Dynamics of Bureaucracy*. Univ. Chicago Press, Chicago, 1963.

(7) Harrison, P. M. *Authority and Power in the Free Church Tradition*. Princeton Univ. Press, Princeton, New Jersey, 1959.

(8) Peabody, R. L. *Organisational Authority*. Atherton Press, New York and London, 1964.

(9) Sills, D. *The Volunteers*. The Free Press, Glencoe, Illinois, 1957.

(10) Silverman, D. *The Theory of Organisations*. Heinemann, London, 1970.

(11) Roethlisberger, F. J. and Dickson, W. J. *Management and the Worker*. Cambridge Univ. Press, Harvard, 1939.

(12) Likert, R. *New Patterns of Management*. McGraw-Hill, New York, 1962.

(13) Rice, A. K. *The Enterprise and its Environment*. Tavistock Publications, London, 1963.

(14) Parsons, T. A Sociological Approach to the Theory of Organisations. In *Structure and Process in Modern Societies*. Free Press, Glencoe, Illinois, 1960.

(15) March, J. G. *Handbook of Organisations*. Rand McNally & Co., New York, 1965.

(16) Smith, G. op. cit. 1970.

(17) Seeley, J. The Making and Taking of Problems. *Soc. Problems*, *XIV*, 1966.

(18) Albrow, M. The Study of Organisations – Objectivity or Bias? In Gould, J. (Ed.), *Penguin Social Science Survey*, Penguin Books, Harmondsworth, 1968.

(19) Ibid.

(20) Thomas, W. I. *The Unadjusted Girl*. Ginn, Boston, 1923.

(21) Thomas, W. I. *The Child in America*. Knopf, New York, 1928.

(22) Berger, P. and Luckman, T. *The Social Construction of Reality*. The Penguin Press, London, 1967.

(23) Strauss, A. L. *et al*. *Psychiatric Ideologies and Institutions*. Free Press, Glencoe, Illinois, 1964.

(24) Ibid.

(25) Mauksch, H. O. It Defies all Logic – But a Hospital does Function. *Modern Hospital*, 95, 4, 67, 1960.

(26) Pfiffner, J. N. and Sherwood, F. P. *Administrative Organisation*. Prentice-Hall Inc. Englewood Cliffs, New Jersey, 1960.

(27) Harland, D. A Hospital System Model. *Nursing Research*, 12, 4, 272, 1963.

(28) Argyris, C. *Diagnosing Human Relations in Organisation: a case study of a hospital*. Yale University, New Haven, 1956.

(29) Engel, G. V. The Effects of Bureaucracy on the Professional Auto-
      nomy of the Physician. *J. Health & Social Behaviour*, 10, 1, 30, 1969.
(30) Mauksch, H. O. Organisational Context of Nursing Practice in Davis,
      F. (Ed.), *The Nursing Profession*. John Wiley & Sons, New York, 1966.
(31) Wilensky, H. L. The Dynamics of Professionalism. The case of
      hospital administration. *Hospital Administration*, 1, 6, 1962.
(32) Mechanic, D. Sources of Power of Lower Participants in Complex
      Organisations. *Administrative Science Quarterly*, 7, 3, 349, 1967.
(33) Cartwright, A. *Human Relations and Hospital Care*. Routledge & Kegan
      Paul, London, 1964.
(34) Etzioni, A. op. cit. 1964.
(35) Strauss, A. L. *et al*. op. cit. 1964.
(36) Perrow, C. Goals and Power Structures – a historical case study. In
      Freidson, E. (Ed.), *The Hospital in Modern Society*, Free Press, Glencoe,
      Illinois, 1963.
(37) Smith, H. L. Two Lines of Authority are One Too Many. *Modern
      Hospitals, LXXXIV*, 59, 1955.
(38) Freidson, E. *Profession of Medicine: a study of the sociology of applied
      knowledge*. Dodd, Mead, New York, 1972.
(39) Hall, O. Some Problems in the Provision of Medical Services.
      Canadian J. of Econ. & Pol. Sci., XX, 456, 1954.
(40) Cohen, G. L. *What's Wrong with Hospitals?* Penguin Books, Har-
      mondsworth, 1964.
(41) Goffman, E. *Asylums*. Anchor Books, Doubleday & Co., New York,
      1961.
(42) Ibid.
(43) Wing, J. K. Institutionalisation in Mental Hospitals. *Brit. J. Soc.
      Clin. Psychol.*, 1, 38, 1962.
(44) Ley, P. and Spelman, M. S. *Communicating with a Patient*. Staples
      Press, London, 1967.
(45) Ibid.
(46) Waitzkin, H. and Stoeckle, J. The Communication of Information
      about Illness: clinical, sociological and methodological considerations.
      Adv. Psychosom. Med., 8, 180, 1972.
(47) Ley, P. and Spelman, M. S. op. cit. 1967.
(48) Bird, B. *Talking with Patients*. Lippincott, Philadelphia, 1955.
(49) Medical Defense Union and Royal College of Nursing. *Memorandum
      on steps to be taken to avoid the risk of an operation being performed on the
      wrong patient, side, limb or digit*. Royal College of Nursing, London,
      1961.
(50) Skipper, J. K. (Jnr.) and Leonard, R. C. (Eds.) *Social Interaction and
      Patient Care*. Lippincott, Philadelphia, 1965.
(51) Lederer, H. How the Sick view their World. *J. of Social Issues, 8, 4*,
      1952.

(52)   Skipper, J. K. (Jnr.). Mothers' Distress over their Children's Hospitalisation for Tonsillectomy. *J. Marriage and the Family, 18, 45,* 1966.

(53)   Robinson, D. Mothers' Fear their Children's Well-Being in Hospital and the Study of Illness Behaviour. *Brit. J. Prev. Soc. Med., 22, 4, 228,* 1968.

(54)   Escalona, S. Emotional Development in the First Year of Life. In Senn, M. J. E. (Ed.), *Problems of Infancy and Childhood,* Foundation Press, New Jersey, 1953.

(55)   Stacey, M. *et al. Hospitals, Children and their Families.* Routledge & Kegan Paul, London, 1970.

(56)   Moore, W. and Tumin, M. Some Social Functions of Ignorance. *Amer. J. Sociol. 56, 41,* 1949.

(57)   Skipper, J. K. (Jnr.). Communication and the Hospital Patient. In Skipper, J. K. (Jnr.) and Leonard, R. C. op. cit. 1965.

(58)   Wessen, A. Hospital Ideology and Communication between Ward Personnel. In Jaco, E. G. (Ed.), *Patients Physicians and Illness,* Free Press, Glencoe, Illinois, 1958.

(59)   Pill, R. M. Space and Social Structure in Two Children's Wards. *Soc. Rev., 2, 179,* 1967.

(60)   Stacey, M. *et al.* op. cit. 1970.

(61)   Wilson, A. M. T. *Notes on a Background Survey and Jobs Analysis.* Tavistock Publications, London, 1954.

(62)   Cartwright, A. op. cit. 1964.

(63)   Mechanic, D. Role Expectations and Communications in the Therapist-Patient Relationship. *J. Health & Soc. Behaviour, 2, 194,* 1961.

(64)   Stacey, M. *et al.* op. cit. 1970.

(65)   Oppenheim, A. N. *Questionnaire Design and Attitude Measurement.* Heinemann, London, 1966.

(66)   For further discussion see basic texts such as Moser, C. *Survey Methods in Social Investigation.* Heinemann, London, 1958 and Sellitz, C., Jahoda, M., Deutsch, M. and Cook, S. W. *Research Methods in Social Relations.* Holt, New York, 1959. And for a comprehensive critical analysis of the questionnaire approach to the study of social action. Cicourel, A. V. *Method and Measurement in Sociology.* Free Press, Glencoe, Illinois, 1964.

(67)   Oppenheim, A. N. op. cit. 1966.

(68)   Morris, J. N. *Uses of Epidemiology.* 2nd Ed. E. & S. Livingstone, Edinburgh and London, 1964.

(69)   Oppenheim, A. N. op. cit. 1966.

(70)   Weber, M. Economy and Society. (Wirtschaft und Gesellschaft) First part (trans.) Henderson, A. M. and Parsons, T. as *The Theory of Social and Economic Organisation.* New York, 1947.

Chapter VII.   Sociology and the Provision of Medical Care
(1)   McLachlan, G. (Ed.). *Problems and Progress in Medical Care*. Oxford University Press, London, 1966.
(2)   Ibid.
(3)   Sigerist, H. E. *A History of Medicine*. Oxford University Press, London, 1951.
(4)   Bullough, V. L. The Term "Doctor". *J. of the History of Medicine and Applied Sciences*, XVIII, 284, 1963.
(5)   Rosen, G. The Hospital: Historical Sociology of a Community Institution. In Freidson, E. (Ed.), *The Hospital in Modern Society*. Free Press, New York, 1963, and Abel-Smith, B., *The Hospitals: 1800–1948*. Heinemann, London, 1964.
(6)   Garrad, J. and Rosenheim, M. *Social Aspects of Clinical Medicine*. Baillière Tindall and Cassell, London, 1970.
(7)   Fordar, A. (Ed.). *Penelope Hall's Social Services of England and Wales*. Routledge & Kegan Paul, London, 1969, and Titmuss, R. M. *Essays on the Welfare State*. Unwin University Books, London, 2nd Edn., 1970.
(8)   Jefferys, M. *An Anatomy of Social Welfare Services*. Michael Joseph, London, 1965.
(9)   Straus, R. The Nature and Status of Medical Sociology. *Amer. Sociol. Rev.*, 22, 200, 1957.
(10)   Robinson, D. Becoming an Alcoholic: notes on a study of procedural definitions. *J. of Alcoholism*, 8, 2, 1973.
(11)   Butterfield, W. J. H. and Wadsworth, M. E. J. A London Teaching Hospital. In LcLachlan, G. (Ed.) op. cit. 1966.
(12)   Pattison, E. M. A Critique of Alcoholism Treatment Concepts with Special Reference to Abstinence. *Quart. J. Stud. Alc.*, 27, 49, 1966.
(13)   Blane, H. T. *et al.* Social Factors in the Diagnosis of Alcoholism. *Quart. J. Stud. Alc.*, 24, 640, 1963.
(14)   Meador, C. K. The Art and Science of Non-Disease. *New England J. of Medicine*. CCLXXII, 92, 1965.
(15)   Robinson, D. op. cit. 1973.
(16)   Bastide, R. *The Sociology of Mental Disorder*. (Trans. McNeil, J.) Routledge & Kegan Paul, London, 1972.
(17)   Lofland, J. *Analysing Social Settings*. Prentice-Hall, Englewood Cliffs, New Jersey, 1971.
(18)   Cicourel, A. V. *Method and Measurement in Sociology*. Collier Mac-Millan, London, 1964.
(19)   Lofland, J. op. cit. 1971.
(20)   Roth, J. *Timetables*. Bobbs-Merrill, Indianapolis, 1963.
(21)   McCall, G. and Simmons, J. L. (Eds.). *Issues in Participant Observation: A text and reader*. Addison-Wesley Publishing Co., Reading,

Mass., 1969. Denzin, N. K. *The Research Act: A theoretical introduction to sociological methods*. Aldine Publishing Co., Chicago, 1970.
(22) Lofland, J. op. cit. 1971.
(23) Fox, R. C. *Experiment Perilous: physicians and patients facing the unknown*. Free Press, Glencoe, Illinois, 1959.
(24) Jefferys, M. Sociology and Medicine: Separation or symbiosis? *Lancet*, i, 1111, 1969.

AUTHOR INDEX

Abel-Smith, B., 140, 167, 171
Albrow, M., 116, 117, 168
Anderson, J. A. D., 167
Anderson, O., 165
Apple, D., 47, 164
Argyris, C., 168

Balint, M., 48, 72, 85, 163, 165
Bastide, R., 65, 85, 164, 165, 171
Becker, H. S., 88, 99, 109, 161, 165, 166, 167
Berger, P., 18, 168
Bird, B., 128, 169
Blane, H. T., 144, 171
Blau, P. M., 168
Bloom, S. N., 166
Bottommore, T. B., 161, 166
Briggs, A. E., 167
Brock, Lord, 102, 167
Bullough, V. L., 140, 171
Burton, R., 96, 166
Butterfield, W. J. H., 142, 171

Cahalan, D., 166
Caplow, T., 91, 102, 166, 167
Cartwright, A., 132, 169, 170
Christ, E. A., 167
Cicourel, A. V., 160, 170, 171
Clyne, M. G., 164
Cobb, S., 64, 163
Cochrane, A. L., 165
Coe, R. M., 28, 161, 162
Cogan, M. L., 92, 110, 166
Cohen, G. L., 123, 169
Cook, S. W., 170
Coser, R. L., 138, 161
Coulson, M. A., 18
Crocker, L. H., 162
Cushing, H., 165

Davis, F., 110, 167, 169

Denzin, N. R., 166, 172
Deutsch, M., 170
Di Cicco, L., 164
Dickinson, W. J., 168
Douglas, J., 23, 162
Dubos, R., 46, 163
Duff, S., 71, 165
Durkheim, E., 2, 16, 161, 162

Edmunds, V., 167
Edwards, G., 25, 162
Engel, G. V., 169
Escalona, S., 130, 170
Etzioni, A., 111, 112, 113, 167, 168, 169

Feldstein, P. J., 97, 166
Field, M. G., 166
Flerner, A., 165
Fordar, A., 171
Fox, R. C., 66, 75, 156, 157, 160, 164, 165, 172
Freeman, H. E., 161, 163
Freidson, E., 70, 71, 72, 85, 87, 94, 109, 110, 122, 138, 164, 165, 166, 167, 169, 171

Garland, L. H., 80, 165
Garrad, J., 171
Gibson, Q., 42, 163
Glueck, B. C., 163
Goffman, E., 125, 138, 165, 169
Gomberg, W., 86, 163
Goode, W. J., 92, 93, 94, 166
Gordon, G., 63, 163, 164
Gould, J., 168
Gulick, L., 167

Habenstein, R. W., 167
Hall, O., 169
Hall, P., 171
Harland, D., 168

Harrison, P. M., 168
Henderson, A. M., 161, 164, 170
Hensman, C., 164
Hinkle, L. E., 163
Hippocrates, ix, 161
Hollander, M. H., 70, 71, 72, 164
Hollingshead, A. B., 71, 165
Howe, G. M., 163
Hyde, D. R., 166

Inkeles, A., 162
Ireland, Father John, 161

Jackson, D. M., 103, 167
Jaco, E. G., 170
Jahoda, M., 170
Jefferys, M., 159, 160, 171, 172
Jellinek, E. M., 162

Kahn, J. H., 106, 167
Kasl, S. V., 64, 163
Keller, M., 162
Kitsuse, J., 160
Knutson, A., 164
Koch, R., 28
Kosa, J., 19, 162
Koos, E., 66, 83, 85, 87, 164, 165

Lederer, H., 169
Leonard, R. C., 165, 169, 170
Lerner, M., 165
Levinson, D. J., 100, 167
Ley, P., 125, 126, 127, 128, 138, 169
Likert, R., 168
Lofland, J., 152, 155, 160, 171, 172
Luckmann, T., 168
Lynd, R., 17, 162

MacCarthy, D., 9, 161
McCall, G., 171
McLachlan, G., 139, 171
McNeil, J., 164

Mandelbaum, D. G., 162
March, J. G., 168
Margolis, P., 163
Mauksch, H. O., 119, 168, 169
Meador, C. K., 81, 165, 171
Meadow, S. R., 9, 161

Mechanic, D., 19, 47, 48, 68, 83, 86, 161, 162, 163, 164, 165, 169, 170
Merton, R. K., 110, 166
Mettlin, C. J., 166
Moore, W., 170
Morris, J. N., 47, 162, 170
Moser, C., 170
Mulford, H. A., 24, 162

Oppenheim, A. N., 134, 135, 170
Ostler, Sir W., 75, 76, 165

Pareto, V., 77
Parsons, T., 52, 54, 58, 59, 63, 64, 74, 77, 161, 163, 164, 165, 168, 170
Pattison, E. M., 144, 171
Paul, J. R., 162
Peabody, R. L., 168
Pearce, I. H., 162
Perrow, C., 121, 169
Pfiffner, J. N., 168
Phillips, B. S., 166
Phillipson, R. V., 162
Pill, R. M., 170

Reader, G. G., x, 161
Rex, J., 4, 161
Rice, A. K., 168
Riddell, D. S., 18
Riley, D., 9, 161
Roberts, M., 167
Robinson, D., 47, 162, 163, 164, 165, 170, 171
Roche, P., 56, 164
Roemer, M. I., 64, 163
Roethlisberger, F. J., 168
Rosen, G., 140, 171
Rosenheim, M., 171
Roth, J. A., 72, 153, 165, 171

Scheff, T., 76, 80, 165
Schneider, D., 164
Schumacher, C. F., 166
Scorer, C. G., 167
Seeley, J., 25, 116, 162, 168
Sellitz, C., 170
Selznick, P., 38, 163
Senn, M. J. E., 170

Sharaf, M. R., 100, 167
Sherwood, F. P., 168
Short, D. S., 167
Shostak, A. B., 86, 163
Sigerist, H. E., 52, 64, 140, 160, 163, 166, 171
Sills, D., 168
Silverman, D., 115, 138, 168
Simmons, J. L., 171
Skipper, J. K., Jnr., 75, 130, 132, 165, 169, 170
Smith, A., 111, 112
Smith, G., 113, 168
Smith, H. L., 122, 169
Snow, Sir J., 28
Spelman, M. S., 125, 126, 127, 128, 138, 169
Stacey, M., 161, 170
Stevens, R., 166
Stoeckle, J., 126, 128, 169
Straus, R., 140, 141, 160, 171
Strauss, A. L., 118, 120, 168, 169
Suchman, E. A., 70, 71, 72, 164
Szasz, T., 35, 163

Thomas, W. I., 117, 168
Titmuss, R. M., 171
Tumin, M., 170
Twaddle, A. C., 64, 163

Urwick, L., 167

Virchow, R., 1, 161

Wadsworth, M. E. J., 142, 171
Waitzkin, H., 126, 128, 169
Weber, M., 3, 4, 17, 50, 65, 66, 161, 162, 164, 170
Wessen, A., 132, 170
Wilensky, H. L., 169
Wilson, A. M. T., 170
Wilson, L., 166
Wing, J. K., 24, 125, 162, 169
Wootton, B., 56, 164
Worsley, P., 18

Zacune, J., 164
Zborowski, M., 164
Zola, I. K., 47, 86, 107, 163, 167

SUBJECT INDEX

Addictions, 57–58
Alcohol problems, referral for, 143–154
Alcoholic, becoming an, 22–26, 106–107, 143–154
Alcoholism, diagnosis of, 143–154
"offered" diagnosis of, 145
potential diagnosis of, 143, 145
"private" diagnosis of, 147
American Sociological Association, x
Authority, bureaucratic, 122
conflict between types of, 123–124, 138
formal administrative, 122
professional, 122
two lines of, in hospital, 122, 138

Becoming ill, the process of, 19–47
British Sociological Association, x
Buerger's disease, 44

Children in hospital, 8–10
Clinical experience, 99
Clinical "iceberg", 33–35, 47
Communication, barriers to, 126–127
the "problem" of, 125–129
unhelpful assumptions about, 127–129
Correspondence, between hospital and G.P.'s, 145–147

Decision-making to "clear the air", 38–39, 41, 42, 77–80
Defining the situation, 117–118
Definitions, taken-for-granted, 25, 87
Desire to get well, 58–61, 63
Deviance, legal and medical responses to, 55–57
Doctor, evaluation by patient, 68–69
role of, 37–38, 77
two facets of role of, 68

Doctor-patient relationship, ix, 43, 65–85
activity-passivity of, 70–72
typology of, 70–72
Doctors and patients, as experts and laymen, 69–70
differing conceptions of illness of, 67
differing priorities of, 43, 67, 69, 82
Drama analogy, 6, 14, 17–18

Emergency admissions committees, 123
Epidemiologic method, 28
Everyday sociology, 15, 16, 23
Expectations of other's actions, 3, 4, 6, 13, 17, 26, 36, 52, 66
Experts, non traditional medical, 83–84

General Medicine Council, ix

Healers, folk, 84
spiritual, 84
Health diary, 39–42, 78–79
Health surveys, 29–33, 34, 49
Help-seeking, 61–63
Hippocratic code, 101, 102
corpus, ix
Hospitals, and general practice, 124
as complex organizations, 111–138
as negotiated orders, 120–121
dominant group policies in, 121–122
viewed from various perspectives, 119–120

Illness, symptoms of as statistical norm, 34
Illness behaviour, 19–20, 48
defined, 19
Illness conditions, and ageing, 60–61
and concomitant behaviour, 19, 46, 48, 63
and sociology, 20–26, 46

differential exposure to, 27–29
differential responses to, 35–46
incidence of, 29
multi-causality, 35
prevalence of, 29
the question of responsibility for, 54–58, 63
Information, and mother's distress, 130
satisfaction with, and social class, 131–133
satisfaction with and source of, 132–133
satisfaction within hospital, 129–134
Interaction in treatment, as negotiation, 72

Man, over socialized conception of, 62
singularity of, 62
Medical activities, interrelatedness of, 139–142
Medical decision-rules, 80–81
Medical education, xi, 98–100
Medical emergency, 122–123
Medical ethics, 101–103
Medical professional, autonomy of, 96–98, 109, 122
evaluation of, 100–101
Medical recruitment, 98–100
Medical responsibility, 99, 104, 105, 109
Medical sociology, tasks of, 38, 41, 43, 45
Medical student, as potential man of action, x, 99–100
Medicine, and the market place, 97–98
as a dominant occupation, 95
as a profession, 87–110
as an institution of social control, 106–109
as applied knowledge, 96
as synthesis of many disciplines, x
control over, 100–103
division of labour in, 88
M'naughten rule on legal insanity, 55, 56
Mother's role, conflict over, 6, 7–8, 9–10

"Non-diseases", 80–82, 85
"Non-medical" problems, 82–83, 85

Nurses, claims for professional status by, 105–106, 109

Obesity, types of theory of, 21–22
Observations, known and unknown, 153–159
Observer's role, 154–155
Occupational prestige scales, 90–92
underlying assumptions of, 91
Occupations, and social class categories, 90–91
definiteness of, 90
prestige of, 89–92
Organizational goals, 112, 113, 114, 137
defined by participants, 115–116
Organizational rules, 113, 118–119, 137
Organizations, 111–134
division of labour in, 111–113
environmental context of, 114–115
"higher participants" in, 116, 137, 155
multiple goals of, 114
realistically defined, 117–119
traditionally defined, 111–117
unity of control in, 112
Patient, and doctor, ix, 43, 65–85
by conscious choice, 68
social position of, 26, 36, 47, 48–64
temporary occupancy of social position of, 59–60, 81
Platt committee report, 9, 10
Privileged access, by doctor, 73–74, 85
Probation officers, 148–151
Profession, difficulty over definition of, 84
notion of, as social symbol, 88
Professional, autonomy of, 94
notion of, 87
Professionals and para professionals, 103–106, 109
Professions and other occupations, 87–95
crucial distinction between, 94–95
Professions, suggested characteristics of, 93–94

Questionnaire-based studies, 134–137
crucial weakness of, 136–137, 153, 158–159

Questionaire-based studies–*cont.*
  sources of error in, 135–136
  alternatives to, 134, 153–159

Referral, 100–101, 141–152
  from medical sources, 142–146
  from non-medical sources, 147–152
Royal Commission on Medical Education, ix

Sick-role, 52–63, 64
Significant others notion of, 50–51
Social action, 3–4, 13, 17, 51–52, 55, 84, 87, 141
  defined, 3
Social categories, 11
Social groups, 11–14, 18
  defined, 11
Social positions, 5, 18, 66
Social relations, 4–5, 64, 153
  defined, 4
Social responsibilities, exemption from, 52–54, 63
Social roles, 5–11
  and drama analogy, 6, 14, 17–18

Sociological enterprise, xi
Sociologist's task, 53–54, 59, 136, 144, 159
  in the medical school, xi
  in illness situations, 152–159
Sociologist's viewpoint, xiv, 1–18
Sociology, and common-sense, 14, 15–16
  and medicine, xi, xii, 46, 140–141, 159
  as a social science, 2–3
  books for the medical student, xiii
  of occupations, 89, 109
  what it isn't, 16–17
Specialist language, 1–2
Statistical aggregates, 11
Surveys, the question of representativeness, 29–33
  the problem of refusals, 32–33

Total institutions, 124–125

Uncertainty, 74–80, 85
  In the doctor-patient relationship, 76–77